Property Developing & HMO Investment Success

Treating Tenants as clients and working with a conscience

Ersin Sirer

Make your life a masterpiece;
imagine no limitations on what
you can be, have or do

- Brian Tracy
Canadian American
motivational public speaker

Published by
www.elitepublishingacademy.com

First Edition published 2020
© Ersin Sirer

Printed and bound in Great Britain by
www.elitepublishingacademy.com

A catalogue record for this book
is available from The British Library
ISBN 978-1-912713-80-6

Authors Disclaimer & Caveat: I am not qualified to give financial or legal advice. All related recommendations made in this book should only be considered in consultation with suitably qualified and accredited professionals. Persons giving financial advice MUST be properly qualified and regulated by the Financial Conduct Authority (FCA) and anyone giving you legal advice should be qualified and regulated by The Law Society and the Solicitors Regulation Authority or the Council of Licensed Conveyancers. I add the caveat that all third-party information, i.e. loan interest, loan arrangement fees, loan to value percentages, HMO license regulations and minimum room sizes, any planning laws are all subject to change, therefore should be checked before entering into property investing and developing.

Table of Contents

PROPERTY DEVELOPING

Houses of Multiple Occupation

Property General

Dedication

To my wonderful caring wife Fatiha and my kids Reem & Kerim. I am grateful and honoured for your love, and to my late father for being my inspiration to work hard with honesty and decency.

I also dedicate this book to those millions of people without a roof over their heads, living on two dollars a day, and the silent world majority who live in sub-standard homes because of sheer greed and the shameless lack of care and responsibility of landlords.

Foreword

From a family deeply rooted in the development industry – in residential property, mining and cultural heritage through to conservation, and for several decades a town planner and consultant, I have observed how UK property sector has evolved to become one of the most sophisticated and internationally recognised investment hubs.

I am honoured to have been invited to write this Foreword for a book from a seasoned property developer that covers property in its every aspect of investing, developing and all associated subject matter such as funding, planning, financials, choosing the right professionals, and HMO developing. Its foundation is conducting business in an ethical way, treating tenants as clients, building positive and credible relationships, homelessness and how to eradicate it.

Investing with a conscience is where one thinks of the impact of that investment and how it will impact society, tenants, end users and the environment. Ersin's emphasis is on conducting business in a morally upstanding way. These principles top the curve of current business practice and which we know is breaking into mainstream when it begins to be reported in the national and technical press.

Slum landlords and unethical developers are slowly on the way out. This space is changing, society's expectations from business people have risen, Ersin is at the forefront of these changes and is setting an example.

The winners in all aspects of any industry will be those who are prepared. If we are to do this, as Ersin Sirer affirms 'We need to invest in an ethical way thinking of the environment and society at large.' And this book is one of the beginnings.

Clare B Wright MRTPI MILM
Chartered Town Planner
Director, C.B.Wright & Associates Ltd

My Late Father

My beloved late father came from a village in North Eastern Turkey on the Black Sea coast next to Georgia. He was born to illiterate parents, the eldest of 6 siblings, they were so poor that he was sent to Istanbul at the age of 11 to work to help support the family financially. His first job was as a bellboy in a hotel.

My father was a highly intelligent person, he always wanted to study and go to university, but never had the opportunity to do so, therefore all his adult life he read profusely, thousands of books, his desire to educate himself continued until the day he died. A credible and inspirational man, hardworking, ethical and kind, never raised his voice and respected everyone. He was ambitious and within a few years of his arrival in the UK in 1969 he had set up the first Turkish restaurant chain in London, with the exception of a major heart attack at the age of 42 he worked non-stop for 69 years. He helped many people with wisdom and advice, financially, and business guidance. At his funeral on 27th December 2017, hundreds turned up and he was buried by his ex-staff, some who had worked for him over 30 years ago.

His quiet determination to do better and to never give up are the same character traits that most successful entrepreneurs and people have. To reach one's objective is key in any long-term life strategy whatever one's vocation, but along the way we must reach out to give to and help others better their lives.... Thank you, "Baba", (Dad in Turkish), for showing me the way.

Vision for Leadership in Business

The ethical leader understands that positive relationships are the gold standard for all organizational effort. Good quality relationships built on respect and trust—not necessarily agreement. The ethical leader understands that these kinds of relationships germinate and grow in the deep rich soil of fundamental principles: *trust, respect, integrity, honesty, fairness, equity, justice* and *compassion*.

Early last century the German philosopher and theologian, Martin Buber, described these successful relationships as *"I-Thou"* relationships, in which people recognize the intrinsic worth and value of others and treat each other with sincerity and respect. In the language of the 18th century German philosopher, Immanuel Kant, this is the principle of always treating the other person as an *end* and never merely as a *means* to serve your own personal interests. The ethical leader moves and acts in a world of I-Thou relationships, where in any situation, to the fullest extent possible in the circumstances, the intent is to honour and respect the worth of the other person.

- **Don't separate ethics from day-to-day business**: Business people must make it clear to their employees that ethics is "the way we operate" and not a training program or reference manual. Every activity, whether it is a training program, a client meeting or an important top management strategy session, should include conversations about ethics.
- **Don't think about ethics as just following laws and regulations**: Business people need to take action and show consumers and other stakeholders that they are actively engaged with ethical issues that matter. Recognize how ethics influences consumers' reasons to buy from you and demonstrate a commitment to go beyond mere compliance with laws and regulations.

- **Don't exempt anyone from meeting ethical expectations:** Allow no excuses. Make sure that no one is exempted from meeting the ethical standards that are adopted. Maintain the status of ethics as a total, absolute, "must do" in the organization. Hold everyone, particularly senior leaders and high-profile managers, accountable.

- **Celebrate positive ethical moments:** Be a proactive ethical business person, championing high ethical conduct and emphasizing prevention.

- **Talk about ethics as an ongoing learning journey.**

We must accept that every business decision and action we take has a consequence, the consequence must not just be profit with the motto that more is better. We need to consider how it will affect our fellow human, be they employees, tenants, neighbours, business partners and all, this outlook will enable us to move in the right direction, leading to a fairer and more just society.

About the Author

A property developer with a conscience?

Yes, that's me.

Strange as it may sound, but there are some of us out there.

In a business and industry littered with sharks, cowboys and conmen, I believe there is a better way to operate. Guidelines to stick to, rules and regulations to adhere to...and a general ethos that treats tenants as clients but also makes an average landlord both a 'profitable and responsible landlord'. Win win!

I hope this book will show you how, from humble beginnings, I was able to build my property portfolio through a measured and conscientious approach. Along the way I constructed and developed some wonderfully unique high-end luxury properties and converted offices to flats too.

Focusing on my well-honed know-how of operating as an HMO (Houses of Multiple Occupancy) landlord, this book will also show how, as Turkish immigrants arriving in London in the late 1960s, my father's hard-work ethics and business acumen inspired my own businesses career.

Helping my father set up our first fast food outlet in central London in the early 1980s in my late teens gave me the hunger for more.

As the family business opened more cafes and restaurants, I evolved through the process and quickly wanted to set up on my own business.

When we started to acquire freeholds, including the accommodation above the units, the concept of being a landlord myself was born.

I had completed a diploma in business at college, but that could hardly prepare me for the cut -throat landscape of property developing. I have always considered myself largely self-taught in that regard.

My considered and thorough approach has taken me from initial Assured Shorthold Tenancies (ASTs), single unit residential rental investments to multiple developments in the Prime London Sector (PLS) in areas like Kensington & Chelsea and New Build Luxury Houses (NBLH) in exclusive suburbs in Surrey.

Through my network of credible business people, I source and Joint Venture with other reputable property developers. This is the Capital Partners segment of my business activities and allows me to reach out into areas of UK and participate in projects which otherwise I would not be able to do. It's all about sharing the risks and the rewards.

I have also ventured out of the UK, organising and creating a syndicate of like-minded independent partners investing in overseas property.

Today my core business is HMOs…and it's taken me to provincial towns like Eastbourne, Swindon, Chippenham, Exeter and London too.

Now I want to share my own finely tuned formulas of how to make your own 'House of Multiple Occupation' business both successful and ethical.

Backstory

I was born in Istanbul in the Spring of 1963 and had little schooling in Turkey before my father's job as an assistant general manager at a five-star hotel took us to London six years later.

A business acquaintance of his knew the owner of a hotel just off Gloucester Road London and fixed up a management position for Dad. It was an adventure neither he nor my mother could resist.

In Istanbul we lived in a flat in the mid-suburbs. Not rich not poor. Life was fairly comfortable, but my father was ambitious. And fortunately, he was a saver and good with money. We arrived in London with a few thousand pounds – a hell of a lot of money back then.

Now our home was one of the rooms at the hotel in South Kensington, where my father was given a management position.

In the 5-star hotel where he worked in Istanbul, he had increased occupancy levels to their maximum, a statistic that had helped secure our move to London. Very quickly my father increased the occupancy at his new workplace also to an average of 80%, which is excellent in the hotel industry. Business was good.

Through living at the hotel, I became best friends with the owner's son, who was also Turkish…and is still one of my best pals to this day. Then after nine months it was time for us to finally 'check out' and we moved to a one-bed rented apartment in Newington Green, north London. It wasn't much, but it was home.

Now the family outgoings had increased significantly, every penny counted.

My father worked long hours at the hotel and my mother worked in a supermarket, so I had to wait at an after-school club for her to finish her shift before I could be picked up and taken home.

I was an immigrant with few friends, so I had deep periods of loneliness, always in the corner on my own it seemed. Spending hours each week at school after most kids had gone home, feeling alone, was hard for me. I literally felt backed into a corner, and from an early age I resolved never to treat anyone as insignificant, and never knowingly have.

We started to move around. Next stop a bigger two-bedroomed flat in a Victorian house in North West London when I was eight years old, then a purpose-built two-bedroomed flat close by within the same borough. There are few positive memories from that time in my life. I was still a loner, with not many friends.

At the age of 11 I began secondary school at William Gladstone. It was a troubled school, with a gang culture, and was eventually bulldozed. The toughest kid in our school was beaten up and knifed by a rival gang. My mum and I saved the boy and took him home with us. With bullies like that you either became like them...or showed no fear. I chose the latter.

I also decided to study...and study hard. I became one of the best in my year at school, through sheer hard work. From being bottom of the class at the age of six when I arrived in London, I now had the best grades among my peers in the school. I consistently received high grades and excellent reports, and became a model student, I was personally commended by the headmaster several times.

Then I came crashing back down to earth. I at the age of 14 was present at a parents evening when my bubble was burst. One teacher told Mum and Dad: "It doesn't matter how hard Ersin works, he will never become good at this subject." Those words shattered me, and completely demotivated me. I rebelled from that point on and dropped down a class in all subjects. I was in my mid-teens now, and it seemed it was that time in my life...to rebel.

The fall out meant I didn't get great grades at O-level. My parents were upset and saddened, they still tried to motivate me. My father was very busy and focused on his expanding business activities, and he hadn't been tough enough on me. And, if I am honest, I didn't want to leave school at that point. I actually enjoyed education. So, between the ages of 16 and 17 I stayed on at school and got better grades and continued to College to study Business Administration. If I could turn the clock back, I wouldn't have rebelled, not that I don't agree with rebelling. I think people should do that in certain situations and at various points in their lives. Much of the positive changes we have in society are due to people standing up for their rights and rebelling, thereby bringing improvements to all people.

The pessimist sees difficulty in every opportunity. The optimist sees opportunity in every difficulty

- Winston Churchill

Turkish Army – The Rebel

I am proud to be a British citizen, and believe Great Britain is truly great. This wonderful country has given me and my family so much…safety, education, business opportunities, citizen rights, democracy, excellent free healthcare service and many other things.

Even though I have lived in the UK since I was six years old, I still hold a Turkish passport, and all male Turkish citizens have to do national service.

So, at the age of 38 I went back to Turkey to complete my national military service.

Fortunately, as a non- resident in Turkey, I had the opportunity to do a short version, just weeks, held in a special camp only for Turks living abroad.

However, it is still the army and there is no special treatment given to the soldiers. And, of course, it's a culture shock to most of us who have been living and working in a culture that doesn't insist on compulsory national service.

I love my country of origin, and I love my Turkish culture. I am proud of our history and the Turkish people. I went to the army with idealism and enthusiasm, I was proud and grateful to be there. My experiences were overall positive. We were taught the basics of shooting, marching etc, but within limited timescales.

What I found most fascinating, were the many educational seminars on the history of Turkey. This included the origins of the language. Turkic languages are spoken as a native language by some 170 million people, and the total number of Turkic speakers, including second language speakers, is over 200 million.

While I was in the camp, I noticed that some of the regular army, mainly the lower ranked commanders were not doing their job properly. They were lax and disrespectful towards us.

This upset me tremendously to the point where I lost my temper on one of those occasions, where the commander was being disrespectful to us soldiers.

I believe consideration and respect to others and to ourselves is of paramount importance. This is how I live my life every day and how I carry out my daily responsibilities with others.

It was Autumn and we were told to brush the dried grass and leaves from the ground. However, we were not given suitable equipment to complete this task. Instead, we had to use our feet and shuffle. This was the straw that broke the camel's back for me, added to all the other negative incidents I had witnessed.

I told the sergeant who instructed our platoon to shuffle our feet to brush the dead grass, that I was not going to do, I spoke to him in a forceful but respectful way. Two of my platoon members also did not want to carry out this instruction. The sergeant came up close to me said how dare I not carry out his orders.

I told him how dare he speak to us in a disrespectful way and ask us to shuffle our feet like lunatics.

I pointed out that we had come back to Turkey because we loved our country and wanted to do right by it, by completing our national service. The sergeant then being lost for words asked me and the two others who had disobeyed orders to say it to the face of the Captain who had issued the orders. So, we agreed.

On our way to see the Captain my platoon comrades suggested I didn't speak with the Captain in the same way as I would surely be locked up. I had already decided I would rather face imprisonment than be disrespected in this way.

When I got to the Captain, a person who was disliked by most, he did not even look at me. Perhaps I was not worthy of his attention. He soon found out otherwise. With a loud voice, but still respectfully, I told him that I and my two comrades would not be carrying out his instructions and gave him the reasons why. I made sure all the other soldiers heard exactly what I was saying, I wanted to diminish him and his authority for his shameful disrespect of us soldiers. He was shocked and told me I was not speaking to him in the right way. I responded and told him I did not need him to teach me the art of communication.

What surprised me even more was what happened next. Instead of sending me away for a stint in solitary confinement, the Captain told me to move on and not do what he had instructed. I had won. We were shocked.

I thought about this situation many times afterwards. Why did I get away with it? My assumption is that my communication and body language must have given the commander the impression that I had connections within the army and the camp, which I did not. I was a mere regular, the lowest rank soldier, but the Captain must have feared the consequences that may have befallen him.

I firmly believe that we must stand up for our rights, be it in an army camp or in civil society, and treat all irrespective of their colour, sex, religion, and financial status with respect and consideration. This is how I carry out my personal and business affairs.

Don't let yesterday take up too much of today

- Will Rogers

A Fast Track to Fast Food

My father left the hotel in the early 1970s and opened a Wimpy Bar burger restaurant in Kingsbury in north west London. The first Wimpy, an American brand originally franchised in the UK by Lyons, opened in the UK in the 1950s, and by 1970 there were more than 1,000 Wimpys worldwide.

Armed with years of experience in frontline hospitality and catering, my father seized the opportunity and obtained a Wimpy franchise with a partner, and soon opened a second Wimpy Bar in Harrow Weald. His ambition led him to further expansion opening a Turkish Kebab takeaway in South Kensington in 1974, which still operates to this day. More openings followed with restaurant branches in Notting Hill Gate, St Pauls Cathedral, Blenhiem Street, an upscale restaurant with pianist in Old Brompton Road South Kensington. Soon Dad and his partners had central London's first Turkish restaurant chain.

If it hadn't been for ill health, having suffered a major heart attack at the age of 42, my father would have continued to expand. He was the hardest worker I have ever known, determined to do well…honest, decent and caring for all around him. He never used anyone and never walked over anyone. Dad passed away aged 80 in 2017 at his funeral many ex-staff flocked to pay their respects. Some who had left his employment 30 years previously cried and showed genuine sadness at his passing.

While I was at college in the late '70s I took a part-time job in Wembley at McDonald's. It had clearly been decided I would earn my burger bar apprenticeship elsewhere, or maybe I had just been dispatched to check out the competition.

Of course, McDonalds, a relatively fledgling operation at that stage, would go onto the dominate the fast food sector in the years to come, but not with the help of Ersin Sirer. I was sacked for flipping the burgers too many times. I tried to argue my case, but the manager said: "You are not here to think, you're here to work."

Charming! After being spoken to in that way I left immediately without giving notice.

But most importantly, it did seem now that I was destined to work in the family business, as I quickly landed a position at the Wimpy Bar. A family business, which thankfully allowed you to both think and work.

My father's business was expanding rapidly, and his 19-year-old son was hungry to be more and more involved. After I finished college my father opened a fast food outlet next door to the coach station in Victoria, with me as an 'operations partner'.

As my father had suffered a major heart attack a few years earlier, he was unable to help physically and could not be involved in the day-to-day operations. He still injected the money needed, but I would be the sole operations partner of the restaurant.

I ran it for six months, pretty much as we found it, a tired fast food restaurant dependent on passing trade from the coach station. Then we shut it down and redecorated and re-opened as The Fast Chef. Business soared after the facelift and new branding.

It was a baptism of fire, but I like to think that, when needed, I stepped up to the plate...literally.

This was the early 1980s and I was barely in my 20s. We had around six staff. My management style, with little training, was quite severe, but I was conscious that if I let standards drop or I gave up it would have finished the restaurant and my fledgling career. This was my first big test in business.

I put the time in. We opened at 6am and shut at 11pm. I put in 16-17-hour days and regularly slept in my car, as there was no time to drive back home. I lost 12 kilos in weight literally from the sheer hard work and stress. I looked terrible but felt great, I felt a sense of achievement and purpose.

And business was booming.

And so, we continued to expand. Taking on the leases of more restaurants. We paid high premiums, but back then running a restaurant was a licence to print money. Very few of the big chains around today existed then.

As our expansion continued, I sourced the sites, created the menu, hired and fired the staff, while my father was involved in the financing of the acquisitions.

You learn more from
failure than from success.
Don't let it stop you.
Failure builds character

- Unknown

A Bun in The Oven

In 1984 the UK economy was doing well; house prices were going up and there was lots of optimism in the air. My father's recovery from his heart attack was still in progress and going well, but he was naturally less involved in the day-to-day running of the restaurants. The Fast Chef was going from strength to strength and my management skills were evolving and developing so it seemed the perfect time to invest in our latest project, The Chelsea Bun, just off the King's Road, in Chelsea.

The Chelsea Bun has occupied the same location since the 1950s. Before 1981 it was a smaller building, more a bus café than a fully-fledged eatery. In 1981 it was completely rebuilt to what we have now.

With my father as the investor partner, I slowly re-modelled The Chelsea Bun from a café into a modern brunch-style café/restaurant and rode on a crest of a wave for the rest of the 1980s and 90s.

24

In 1990 we bought a new restaurant, a freehold commercial property in Fulham Road, and, after major build works, re-opened it as a modern fish restaurant called The Mediterranean.

I moved out of the suburbs...to Holland Park, much more central, and closer to The Chelsea Bun and the new restaurant in Fulham.

But the Mediterranean was a challenge. The late 80s recession was beginning to hit, with the Gulf War contributing to the doubling of interest rates in early 1991.

In anticipation of further downturns in business over the coming period, The Fast Chef was sold.

As the freeholders of The Mediterranean we also owned the large maisonette above the restaurant, the first time we had a residential element to one of our outlets. We didn't rent it out in earnest for twelve months, though, instead letting employees have board and lodging there.

Unfortunately, The Mediterranean didn't make the grade, and in 1992 we closed due to lack of business, largely brought on by 'the recession'. However as we owned the freehold, thank God, we leased out the property to others keen to open their own restaurant. We were now landlords ourselves.

The way get started
is to quit talking
and begin doing
- *Walt Disney*

Branching Out on My Own

In 1993, when I had reached the age of 30, I secured a loan, and purchased The Chelsea Bun from my father, and we separated amicably.

It made sense, given Dad's health scare, and because I was hungry to try and make it on my own. By then, I had been in charge of all the operations at the Bun, and for our holding company in general.

My father had provided the finance and the initial administrative infrastructure, and I had learned so much from him.

As I branched out on my own, The Chelsea Bun continued to thrive. In the mid-90s there was still little competition to worry us. At the weekends there would regularly be a queue of customers 40-deep outside. Pop stars and celebrities like Adam Faith, Sir Bob Geldof, Kylie Minogue, Tara Palmer-Tomkinson, Minnie Driver and many others were all regulars.

"Try not to waste your entire life working just to earn a paycheck. Seek to discover what your true passion in life is and start working on turning it into an empire of your own."

- Edmond Mbiaka

In 1996 I purchased a freehold restaurant with two flats above in Battersea, converting the ground floor into a second branch of The Chelsea Bun. After successful planning application, I was able to add a top storey, the flats were gutted completely and redeveloped into three self-contained one-bedroom flats, my first ASTs (Assured Shorthold Tenancies).

There was no stopping The Chelsea Bun brand, and I opened a third restaurant in Ravenscourt Park in 1998. All three sites had exactly the same menu, so that made it easier from an administrative and management point of view. Further expansion continued with a new theme, a Modern British eatery in Chiswick called Gravy in 2001. This was a restaurant/bar concept, great location right in the middle of Chiswick High Road.

But the property bug had got me. Between 1999 – 2004 I developed several residential properties in Fulham. Complete refurbishments where I would reconfigure, increase square footage and create more bedroom space, and then re-sell at a profit. And this was a marker for me...the first time there was no commercial aspect to a property I had bought and sold.

Between 2001 and 2004 I disinvested from the catering business when I sold my share in the Gravy Restaurant and sold Ravenscourt Park and Battersea Chelsea Bun businesses respectively.

Ravenscourt Park I sold on completely, but the Battersea deal was interesting in that I remained the landlord and sold the lease to my manager/chef who worked for me at the time. I got him a loan, started him off in business. I kept the flats, but now had a rental income coming in from the restaurant. The manager who had started up as my washing up person, was now on his way to becoming an operator himself. It was hugely satisfying to help him do that.

Now I was expanding my property portfolio and stepping more and more away from the commercial side of things, albeit my baby, The Chelsea Bun in King's Road remained, I started to look overseas for opportunities.

People who are crazy
enough to think they
can change the world
are the ones who do

- Rob Siltanen

International Property Investing

The key to international investing is thorough investigation and doing your homework properly, finding credible local partners, and checking they are who they say they are. It is easy to be hood-winked into deals which may be presented to you as viable, but in fact are duds and you will not know the difference unless you have studied the market and know all the local dynamics and facts. In 2005 I set up a syndicate of UK partners, who invested, alongside my own funds, into international real estate. I headed the operation and would travel to other countries to follow our investments. I would arrange meetings between my investor partners and local property developers and experts.

I checked out Dubai but didn't think it viable for what I wanted to do. Too many builds going up all over the territory. Too much supply of property, and not enough demand.

Turkey was an obvious target, and with a group of UK-based liked minded co-investors we invested in a strategic new-build project in Istanbul. The project was a success and great experience for all concerned. Within my travels to and from Turkey I met many high-profile developers and even discussed doing a joint venture with the ex-Prime Minister's son, who owned the hotel we stayed at in Istanbul. Soon I had made many high-level business contacts in Turkey: CEOs of large development companies, facilitators in land and portfolio purchases, certified accountants and international construction companies.

Naturally, we looked into other European markets, mainly Eastern Europe, and I began to make strong connections.

I travelled to Poland and the Czech Republic to make contacts and was received very positively. I found local partners, medium to large-sized property developers. I did my due diligence around them, and created a team of professionals, accountants, architects, lawyers, surveyors and agents to facilitate proposed purchases.

Top Tip
The Power of Association

To facilitate my entry into an unknown country and property market I wanted to connect with credible people. An unknown in these markets, I wanted to be taken seriously. Hence, I used a process called The Power of Association.

Through my connections in London I met the European Director of the world's largest title insurance brokers, Stewart Title Guarantee Company. I explained I represented a larger group of investors and we were prospecting real estate in certain European markets.

Next I was introduced to the 'local country director' of Slovakia, and I immediately felt in safe hands. Thereafter I was formally introduced to the best property developers, lawyers, accountants and all manner of connected professionals. I was taken seriously right from the start and I too felt the people I was introduced to were serious players in their given professions and areas of expertise.

This is a very good example of The Power of Association. Because my introduction was through Stewart Title Guarantee Company, the parties I was introduced to could only assume I and my partners were credible too.

Fortunately, I had not officially engaged, or invested, with any of these good people before the 2008 'Great Recession' happened. And I learned from that experience, made some great contacts, which I still have to this day, and hopefully they appreciate that on a mutual basis too.

And while there may have been an economic crash underway, it didn't mean my property ambitions had to be put on hold.

Entrepreneurs are great at
dealing with uncertainty and also
very good at minimizing risk.
That's the classic entrepreneur

- Mohnish Pabrai

The Power of Good Networks

Any business or human activity in the world is about relationships and having the right contacts. This is true in the property sector too.

The projects I have entered, and the different markets I and my investor partners have invested in, are all due to having good contacts, and carrying out thorough due diligence and doing my research and homework.

Good contact networks create great opportunities. However, the knack is knowing when you have met a good contact and using this contact to facilitate either a sale or an introduction to a new opportunity where both the parties' benefit.

On two different occasions my contacts facilitated sale of properties, one in Kensington which was sold for over £2.8 million, and the other a mews property in South Kensington I sold for over £5 million. Both properties were with agents, but I sold them via my business contacts.

Another example is how I entered the HMO market. This was through an introduction to this investment model by the friend of one of my customers at The Chelsea Bun restaurant.

Upon meeting the introducer, I was surprised when he told me how high the returns were. Within a few weeks I had visited the town he had invested in, and within six months, with local assistance and expertise, I had located a house, refurbished and converted it into an operating HMO. I was quickly on my way to building a portfolio of HMOs in different towns and locations. Now I also consult for other investors.

To make a good contact it is important to communicate correctly in a positive way from the outset. This can be as simple as a genuine compliment or the indication that if you do business together you believe he or she will also make money out of the deal. No one in business is going to share with you their knowledge and know-how for free, unless it is a good friend.

Making new contacts and doing business with people is important, but it is equally important to continue the professional relationships you have started. It's not just about doing one deal together but several in the future. Therefore, over a period of time as your base of contacts grow, so does the potential for more opportunities. It's like a tree, as the years pass, the tree gets bigger, there are more branches, the roots are deeper, and the tree is more stable and will not be uprooted easily.

High-End Property Developing

When I came back to investing in the London property market, I started to look at opportunities in my local area. Via my contacts, people on the ground who could identify optimum properties, we started to draw up a shortlist. I needed properties that were un-modernised, and that could be reconfigured. More rooms created, or rooms that could be enlarged. It's all about reconfiguring and optimising the property.

The Prime London Sector (PLS), including Kensington & Chelsea, the borough where The Chelsea Bun and myself were now based, still had strong prospects. My first PLS development was in Queen's Gate, near the Royal Albert Hall, and many others followed in the surrounding areas.

Queen's Gate was a lower-ground floor three-bedroomed apartment, with high ceilings and an internal courtyard/conservatory. We changed the location of the kitchen, so that the room where the kitchen was located became the second bedroom from where you could look into a courtyard type conservatory, and from the conservatory you look into the living room.

It's all about the reconfiguration!

I worked with highly experienced professionals…builders, interior design-led teams who knew exactly what the buyers wanted. I call it 'The Look'… neutral earthy colours with part wooden, part carpeted floors. The key is creating 'a look' which appeals to the widest possible buyer audience.

Part of the sales approach was furnishing the refurbished properties in high-end expensive looking furniture. These would include some very expensive pieces combined with expensive looking but more lower-end budget items, because when you are developing one eye must always be on keeping the costs down. I am selling a lifestyle. Reconfiguring the property into an upmarket home.

In Prime Central London, location is very important, values can vary from street to street and even where the property is located on the street, i.e. is it facing a garden square, is the property on the 1st floor of a Victorian building hence the values can be 20-30% more.

You could have a large two-bedroomed apartment, which will sell in Kensington & Chelsea for multiple millions, but in other towns for a few hundred thousand pounds.

And it's all about being able to change the flow of the property. Not always possible, but with a good architect you can bring him in and let him work his magic. With these projects I worked with professional partners who inputted their expertise into the project to achieve fantastic returns.

Between 2008 and 2014 we worked on multiple developments in Kensington & Chelsea, the last one a mews house in South Kensington where we created a double basement, digging down 9 metres, past the water-table. This house sold for more than £5m. I had several write-ups in national newspapers and in the international press.

In most of these projects I was able to increase the property value by 50% plus, and one such development in much sought-after Phillimore Gardens in Kensington, I purchased at £1.85 million and sold for £3.2 million. That's a 73% increase in value, and the project was completed within 3.5 months. I still had to pay the builders, stamp duty and for materials and provide high quality furniture in a full-furnished and equipped property but done correctly and there was a healthy profit left.

Ensor Mews

Setting a bench mark in double basement conversions, Ensor Mews development project in the heart of South Kensington was the pièce de résistance of my Prime London Developments, there were several national and international newspaper articles about the property. With the creation of two basements the internal area was increased by over 50%, and the clever use of walk-on skylights enabled natural light to filter through to both the 1st and 2nd basements. It sold for over £5 million.

Below photographs of Ensor Mews, South Kensington London SW7.

"THE" MEWS HOUSE

2 ENSOR MEWS SOUTH KENSINGTON SW7

Features

- Air Conditioning / Ventilation
- Zoned Under Floor Heating
- CCTV Video Entry Phone System
- Low Voltage LED Mood Lighting CAT 5
- Steam Shower
- Electric Under Floor Heating to Bathrooms & Master Dressing Room
- Filtered Drinking Water System Incorporated with Boiling Water Tap
- HD TVs Throughout Each Room
- Ceiling Speakers
- Bespoke Wine Room
- Cocktail Bar and Wine Chiller
- Integral Garage with Automatic Remote Door
- Attic Room with Storage
- Echo Fires

Accommodation

- Entrance hall
- Reception room with built in bar
- Reception room/Dining room
- Media room
- Open plan kitchen
- Master bedroom with en suite bathroom, walk in wardrobe and Juliet balcony
- 2 further bedroom suites
- Bedroom 4
- Shower room
- 2 guest cloakrooms
- Utility room
- Wine cellar
- Garage

Articles in National Press about Ensor Mews development, South Kensington, London. Double basement dig-out of 9 metres to create superb quality living space below ground.

Mail On Sunday - Ensor Mews

The hidden world of Mr Chelsea Bun

How the man behind one of London's top celebrity haunts turned a humble mews house into a £6m iceberg home

Daily Express - Ensor Mews

Daily Express Friday September 20 2013   53

expressuk property

To advertise in this section
020 7098 2894 class.property@express.co.uk

Going underground

UPSTAIRS DOWNSTAIRS: The light and spacious living area is in the basement at Ensor Mews in South Kensington, inset, a glass panel fitted into the upper level and, below, owner Erain Sirer

By Andrea Watson

BASEMENTS get a bad press and now people who want to build one face being banned altogether as a result of what some experts regard as ill-informed comment. In November the Government is set to introduce new rules on this type of extension. Applications have soared, particularly in central London areas where property prices are astronomical but also where a basement is often the only possible way to extend.

In areas where there are controls, such as conservation areas, wealthy homeowners are increasingly going underground.

Basement extensions are also getting bigger with some applicants wanting to build three and four storeys underground, so-called iceberg homes.

Two high-profile cases give an idea as to why the public is opposed to basements. In Belgravia, Tetra Pak heir Hans Rausing wants to create a whole new complex with gym, cinema, garage, pool, kitchen and garden under his £70million Grade II listed mansion.

The property consists of three 19th century townhouses and three mews houses and apart from the massive disruption the work will create, there is genuine concern that the fabric of these houses will be weakened.

In Notting Hill, a similarly vast underground extension was successfully opposed by protesters, including Mayor of London Boris Johnson's sister Rachel.

The plan involved excavating public land under the pavement, which they called a "land grab". However, this practice is quite common.

As pressure mounts for tighter controls homeowners are rushing to submit applications for basement extensions before the expected change in planning guidelines. This is of concern to those in the industry.

"Old houses are often not suited to modern lifestyles and the majority of basements are not built for oligarchs but ordinary houseowners like our clients," says Kevin O'Connor, managing director of Cranbrook Basements, who believes that there is a "campaign" against his industry.

He argues that since people often cannot build above their houses it is the only option and believes that it is perverse to prohibit basements.

"The first thing people always mention is the water table but they rarely know the facts. A major study by Arup in 2007 showed that basements have no impact on groundwater."

He also refutes the idea that basement excavations cause disruption, the second issue most often raised by objectors.

"Basements are actually very low energy and green. They answer the needs of people."

Regarding added value, Kevin says this is entirely dependent upon where your property is located. Outside central London, it is unlikely to add value as the costs of excavation tend to start at upwards of £150,000.

"Location is critical," he says. For all that they may be controversial to build, the huge benefit of basements is that their final visual impact is nil. A good example is the work done by Erain Sirer at a mews house in South Kensington.

Erain had few problems over the application for the work submitted in October 2011 and approved six month later.

"There were few objections, with the main one being from someone who wanted to ensure the front door would be in keeping with the existing style," he says.

However, he admits that paperwork alone for this extension cost £35,900 and it is getting worse.

"We were not allowed to work at weekends and it also cost another £30,000 to rent the parking spaces that we needed. We took over all the residential parking slots on one side of the road," he says.

The result is that 2 Ensor Mews has gone from a two-bedroom property into a swish four-bedroom home that is remarkably pleasant, spacious, light and has none of the claustrophobia one might expect from living underground.

Glass panels fitted into the floors at the upper level illuminate the lower levels. The lower level has a bar-cum-wine cellar.

Now on the market with Strutt & Parker priced at £1.2million, Erain expects that clients to be well-heeled single professionals.

"It's a nice house for a younger person and great for parties because any music is not going to disturb the neighbours in the basement," he says.

INFORMATION:
● Cranbrook Basements: www.cranbrook.co.uk 0800 525881;
● Ensor Mews: Strutt & Parker www.struttandparker.com 0207 373 1010

FIVE TIPS TO INCREASE HOME VALUE

ACCORDING to national estate agent Strutt & Parker the top five ways to increase the value of your home are as follows:

1. ROOM TO IMPROVE
Adding an extension is the most costly outlay but could increase the value of your home by up to 20 per cent.

2. TAP INTO HEALTHY RETURNS
The kitchen is the hub of the home. Creating a real asset by modernising it can help you achieve your target asking price.

3. NO REASON TO BLOW HOT AND COLD
The prospect of upgrading a bathroom may deter some buyers but a new bathroom can be a prized asset.

4. SPLASH OUT ON THIS UPGRADE
Installing an en suite or wet room will increase the property's appeal.

5. APPEALING ASPECTS
An attractive garden has been proven to add value to a property.

Ensor Mews - Exclusive London Property

46 | **home** | OPINION

THE SUNDAY TIMES
thesundaytimes.co.uk/home

08.0

What lies beneath

This London mews house has a double one — but is the end nigh for basements?

BEYOND THE BROCHURE

KAREN ROBINSON

What is it with double-glazing companies? If they're a representative microcosm of British business, heaven help us — and the economy. The nation's entrepreneurs can whinge all they want about how they're being held back by a lack of loan funding, employment costs and red tape, but how about pulling their own fingers out first, eh?

OK, this is what happened. In my four-bedroom Victorian terraced house, the mantra is now insulation, insulation, insulation. Which means replacing all the windows with shiny modern ones and ushering in a brave new world of high thermal values and no pesky draughts whistling through rotting woodwork.

So I call six local firms — determined to avoid those national franchises with the daytime telly ads and notorious high-pressure sales techniques — to arrange for them to come round. One never calls back, one never shows up. The other four daily troop round the house (one treads smears of mud into my bedroom carpet) and make helpful, if entirely contradictory, suggestions: two are adamant that it has to be aluminium frames, the other two are all for uPVC. But the follow-up looks like nothing so much as the glazing sector's concerted effort to tell me to sod right off.

After more than a week, I'd had only one estimate, and it took repeated chasing — begging, practically — to extract two more. I'm still waiting for the fourth. One is handwritten; one is typed, but leaves out half my windows, invents a "laundry room" (I wish) and gives no information about the glass to be used. The most professional of the three — with diagrams and glass specifications included — has still managed to slip in a phantom window at £660 plus Vat. Strewth. And I can't help thinking that if I lived in, say, Frankfurt or Warsaw, I could expect a better service.

Anyway, window suppliers can hardly have been top of the list of problems for the developer Ersin Sirer when he was doing up a house on Ensor Mews, in swanky South Kensington — because half of it doesn't have any windows at all. To turn a dinky west London mews house into 2,700 sq ft of living space, Sirer had to dig deep, gouging out two subterranean floors and using all kinds of clever tricks involving mirrors, glass doors and see-through floor panels to squeeze as much daylight as possible down into the depths.

Ensor Mews, London SW7 £5.95m

What you get a 2,700 sq ft mews house in South Kensington, with three bedrooms, a garage and a double basement — but no garden. It was initially priced at £6.7m
Who to call: Savills: 020 7578 9001, savills.co.uk

Extending houses underground is all the rage in the capital's most expensive postcodes. Dubbed, for obvious reasons, the "iceberg", the trend has, frankly, got out of hand. Last month it was reported that a "wealthy hedge fund manager" (who else?) was going to be made to pay nearly £900,000 in fees and charges by the council just for permission to carve out a two-storey, 64m basement under his Notting Hill home.

The plans apparently show more than 10,000 sq ft of subterranean living space, including a swimming pool, a plunge pool, a spa and a wine store. Given the ambitions of the capital's richest homeowners, you wouldn't be surprised to find a skating rink and a livery stable down there.

There were 307 applications for basement extensions in Kensington and Chelsea last year (up from 13 in 2001), yet the council, despite raking in the cash, see above, is going to start clamping down. Sirer, a canny developer — his father was the first person to open a kebab restaurant in London — reckons that means his property is about to acquire rarity value.

He's done out the three-bedroom house in supermart, taupe-à-gogo international-money style, with a few flash features such as a navy blue Rolls-Royce wedged nose to tail in the garage, on the theory that if this behemoth fits, you can get any car in. It has all the high-tech frills, including filtered drinking water, underfloor bathroom heating, ceiling speakers and air con.

The bedrooms on the first floor look out over cul-de-sac on either side. On the ground floor, there's a sitting room and a study, again with windows (not uPVC, I note, but then the energy efficiency rating on the brochure is a could-do-better 50%).

Descending to the upper basement, you find yourself in 700 sq ft of kitchen/living/dining space that flows around an open-tread staircase. Subtle LED lighting and a couple of light wells banish the feeling that you're in a windowless cellar. In the 700 sq ft below this, the decorator has created a chic bar: handy, as it means the lighting can be permanently and appropriately dialled down to cocktail o'clock.

The price has been reduced by £750,000 after an earlier unsuccessful foray into the market, because it turns out that "below zkm fits in better with the area". Who does Sirer think will shell out that much? "Probably a foreigner," he predicts cheerfully, citing the statistic that non-British buyers account for 66% of property sales in Kensington and Chelsea. So welhomme, bienvenue to London SW7, home of the world's poshest basements.

If you would like Karen to cast her critical eye over a property you are selling, email krb@sunday-times.co.uk

The 700 sq ft upper basement, below, has light wells. Left: the kitchen

Below - Phillimore Gardens London W8, sold November 2013 for £3,200,000.

Below - Kensington Court, London W8 – sold November 2013 for £2,812,000.

We may encounter many
defeats but we must
not be defeated

- Maya Angelou

New Build Luxury Homes

After a period of working on 'London Niche Developments' (LND), between 2014 and 2017 I expanded my repertoire and rolled out 'New-Build Luxury Houses' (NBLH) in Surrey.

This is a different model altogether. You buy the land, and need to get planning permission, so it's a much longer project. Once planning is secured, the existing old property (if there is a property on the site) is demolished and you start from the foundation upwards building new homes with a 10-15-year new build warranties.

It's typically a 24-30-month project investment cycle, hence the returns need to be higher as your cash is tied up in the project for longer.

New Build Project – Weybridge Surrey

When developing a new build, it is important to consider two costs which do not come up in developing/reconfiguring existing single units. They are…

CIL

The Community Infrastructure Levy (CIL) is a charge that local authorities can impose on a new development in order to help raise funds which can be used for infrastructure, facilities and services, such as schools or transport improvements, which are needed to support new homes and businesses in the areas.

The CIL is calculated per square metre. The calculation involves multiplying the CIL charging rate by the net chargeable floor area (based on the Gross Internal Area) and also factoring in an index figure to allow for changes in building costs over time.

Section 106 Tax

Section 106 is a legal agreement between an applicant seeking planning permission and the local planning authority, which is used to mitigate the impact of your new home on the local community and infrastructure. It is a tax that can be used to help fund affordable housing as well as roads, parks and youth services.

Affordable Housing

Another very important consideration for developments, is that for projects of 10 or more units they are normally required by the council to make a number of the homes they build officially "affordable"
This number varies across the country but is usually between 30 to 50 per cent and developers will need to be aware of the requirement before they begin drawing up plans.

Merits of New Build

A new home is less likely to have the health concerns or toxic materials of an older home. It can be built with certain materials making it better for the environment. Green and Energy Star rated appliances, and more efficient toilets, plumbing and electrical fixtures allow the build to be green for a more sustainable home in the long run. There is the option to install, sleeve and wire for future technology upgrades, such as home automation and solar. Maintenance costs are lower in the long run as everything is newly built and installed.

Office to Residential Properties

This is often called a PD project, meaning 'Permitted Development'. PD is derived from a general planning permission granted not by the local authority, but by Parliament.

PD rights are a national grant of planning permission, which allow certain building works and changes of use to be carried out without having to make a planning application.

PD is used when you are converting a commercial use property, usually an office or warehouse into residential use. The main fabric and structure of the building cannot be touched, unless for example it can be proven that once build work had started a wall needed to be demolished due to structural and safety issues, this needs to be backed by a structural engineer's report. However, the internals can be completely reconfigured. The flats can be as large or as small as you wish and with any configuration of rooms, this gives the developer a tremendous advantage in building units which are in most demand. Usually with lower-end valued flats these are the 1- & 2-bedroom units and the aim is to cleverly design smaller well configured homes to achieve a competitive edge on your competition.

It's all about reconfiguration!

In a regular planning application process the planners will dictate the size and number of bedrooms each flat will have. Some will be larger flats i.e. 3 bedrooms units, these will be to the detriment of the overall scheme, as large flats will take longer to sell and the price per square foot achieved will be less.

Be aware that any extensions (beyond permitted development) and extra storeys will need planning permission.

This model of property developing is low risk with lower build costs because a functioning building has foundations, with services in place. Usually offices are open plan and therefore stud-wall partitioning can be reconfigured efficiently in a resale market orientated way.

Also, the build period is usually half that of building from ground up, typically 12-15 months for small to medium sized PD conversions.

An office block in Eastbourne is one example of a PD office to residential development I completed relatively quickly. I purchased the property in 2016 and turned into multiple flats, with all units sold in 2017. This was a Victorian building, which was vacant and had office use permission.

Prior to the purchase I did thorough research on the area, including property price comparison, and with my architect looked at prospects of getting a successful change of use from commercial to residential. All my checks proved positive, so I purchased the property at a discounted price of £125 pounds per square feet (psf) and sold at £265 psf. That's over double the original value minus build costs, stamp duty, legal and other development costs.

The scheme involved converting the building into six flats, with a rear extension and reconfiguration of the internals and some structural works.

Due to its proximity to the town centre and the quality finishes, the units were sold quickly.

Restrictions on Permitted Development

In some areas of the country, known generally as 'designated areas', permitted development rights are more restricted. For example, if you live in:

- a Conservation Area
- a National Park
- an Area of Outstanding Natural Beauty
- a World Heritage Site or
- the Norfolk or Suffolk Broads.

You will need to apply for planning permission for certain types of work which do not need an application in other areas. There are also different requirements if the property is a listed building.

The following photographs are completed Office to Residential conversion in Eastbourne of 6 bespoke flats.

We generate fears while
we sit. We overcome
them by action
- Dr Henry Link

Warehouse to Residential Conversions

As I write this book, I am involved in a new development project of a warehouse to residential PD conversion. This is the same PD (Permitted Development) process as with the office to residential. However, not all warehouse conversions work. It does depend on the existing property elevations, windows, and general external structure. Also, the location of the warehouse property is very important. Most warehouses are in commercial estates and a single solitary residential development unit surrounded by commercial warehousing will not work.

This plot is in Hampton Wick, a Thames-side area of the London Borough of Richmond upon Thames. It's gated and right in the centre of an affluent area, two minutes' walk to Hampton Wick station, five minutes' walk to the river and 15 minutes' walk to the shopping hub of Kingston Town centre. The two warehouse buildings will keep the same footprint and structure, there will be some extensions through additional dormer windows and external cladding. We have started to convert the existing two warehouses into eight flats. The completed project will have seven one-bedroom and one two-bedroom flat.

All the units will sell for below £400,000, which is currently the most active segment of the market. They will also qualify for the government-backed Help to Buy Scheme for first-time buyers. This is where the government will fund in London 40% of the value of the property, 20% outside London. The buyer pays 5% and the remaining 55% comes from a bank loan. The buyer will be eligible for the scheme as long as you are in a position to afford a conventional mortgage and have access to a minimum 5% deposit and a first-time buyer. The property you are buying must be a new-build home priced up to £600,000. You won't be able to sublet this home or enter a part-exchange deal on your old home.

This project is a joint venture with a credible and recognized luxury home builder from Surrey. I have a side agreement with the joint venture partner, the construction company will project manage and build on a 'cost no-profit basis' with cost over-run guarantees, we also have a signed JCT Design & Build contract. The plot is owned and financed by my property development company with investor partners. The whole project will be branded with the joint venture partner build brand, therefore giving the units a cache of quality and an upscale lifestyle feel, we will also give a 12 months aftercare warranty. The expected timescale for the build is 9-12 months, with investment timescale 15-18 months. This is a quick turnaround in development timescales as the structure is in situ, with water, waste and electricity supply already existing. Equity and bank development finance is funding the project.

We are forecasting a successful outcome as there is little competition in the area with expected good returns on invested capital.

Proposed Image of Warehouse Conversion

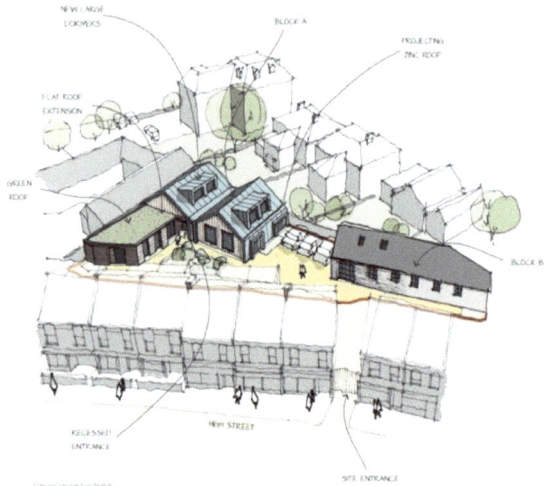

Profit Margins in Property Developing

In the UK professional developers work on a minimum of 20% return on cash, meaning the amount of return on their capital investment without any bank debt. However, with a debt level of circa 75% on total project cost, the return on capital more than doubles to over 54%. If you add further loan funding with a mezzanine second charge debt at an interest of 18% per annum for 10% of the total costs, the returns will go up to 79% return on capital. This is based on a 12-month investment timescale.

Higher return on cash projects usually come with higher risk. These are often larger or longer-term opportunities and ones where there are planning gains, i.e. plots which do not have planning permission and are bought where the purchaser takes on the risk of completing the planning process. These can be with 30-40% return on cash and with bank debt rise to 100% plus return on equity.

EXAMPLE OF RETURNS

The example I have given is of a project with a Loan of 75% to Total Cost and based on 7% interest per annum, with bank arrangement fees at 2%, over an investment timescale of 12 months. This project would have a 20% return on cash without debt. These examples with a debt level of 75% Loan to Total Costs, return on capital increases to 54%, if we borrow a further 10% of costs with a second charge on plot mezzanine loan at 18% interest per annum the return on capital will increase to 79%.

FUNDING EXAMPLES

Example 1 –
PROJECT with 20% Return on Cash

Investment Revenue	£100,000
Total Project Costs (plot purchase & build)	£83,000
Invested Capital	£83,000
Profit	£17,000
Return on Capital	20%

Example 2 –
Bank Debt at 75% of Total Costs (£62,250 borrowed)

Investment Revenue	£100,000
Total Project Costs (plot purchase & build)	£83,000
Project Funding	
Bank Debt	£62,250
Invested Capital	£20,750

Finance Costs & Returns	
Bank Interest Payments	£5,602
(7% interest per annum & 2% arrangement fees)	
Profit	£11,398
Return on Capital	55 %

Example 3 –
Bank Debt @ 75% of Total Costs (£62,250) & Mezzanine Finance for 10% of Project Costs (£8,300) @ 18% per annum interest.

Investment Revenue £100,000

Total Project Costs (plot purchase & build) £83,000

Project Funding
Bank Debt £62,250
Mezzanine Finance £8,300
Invested Capital £12,450

Finance Costs & Returns
Bank Interest Payments £5,602
(7% interest per annum & 2% arrangement fees)
Mezzanine Finance Interest Payments £1,494
(18% per annum interest)
Profit £9,904
Return on Capital 79%

Capital Partners

Another area of my property activities is the 'Capital Partners' business model.

This is where my business partners and I set up a joint venture with another developer or construction company. Through my circle of business contacts, I locate a credible developer/constructor who has experience and local area expertise but is stretched with funding because they are involved with several other projects. Therefore, they are looking for a partner to fund a new venture.

I assess and appraise the project, review the credibility and financial standing of the developer and then agree the joint venture terms. This is the split of profits.

I then agree with the bank "in principle" the lending terms.

The whole deal is then presented to my capital partners.

Once we are all agreed, we proceed to plot purchase, project development, the sale of the completed units and ultimately share of profits. My part of the deal is securing the capital, bank debt and high-level project management (overview of build process and financials). My development company will own the plot and be responsible for all outgoings and any personal debt guarantees. The joint venture partner builds at cost (no profit) and crucially guarantees any cost overruns, brands it with their quality assurance and project manages.

With these ventures the project has to have higher returns as we split profit several ways, but the advantages are they are lower risk, because the build costs are less, and partners are sharing the risk. Crucially, we are using local expertise to branch out into different localities therefore more opportunities are created.

HOUSES OF MULTIPLE OCCUPANCY

HMOs

My main business over the last few years has been the world of the HMO, and, as I explained earlier, I'd like to think that throughout my career as a property developer, I have worked with a conscience and strived to be as responsible as possible. And hopefully maintained competitive profit levels too.

Here's an initial look at how I have applied all my experience and working code of conduct to rolling out HMOs properties.

If you're reading this book as a newcomer to the property business, the first question you may have is: "What exactly is an HMO?"

Well, before I go any further, here's what the Wikipedia listing tells us…

Houses in multiple occupation (HMOs), also known as houses of multiple occupancy, is a British English term which refers to residential properties where 'common areas' exist and are shared by more than one household. Common areas may be as significant as bathrooms and kitchens / kitchenettes but may also be just stairwells or landings.

Now, I'll break it down even further, to the five types of HMOs I come across mostly.

Regular PRS (Private Rental Sector) HMO – a single house divided into self-contained rooms, usually with common bathroom and common living areas.

Large-scale PRS HMO (sometimes come under the title **"Co-Living**) – these would always include en-suite rooms, plus large common areas, restaurant, bar, cinema room, a gym, quiet areas, and a library. The largest I have seen has over 500 en-suited rooms, studios and one bed-room flats.

Student HMO houses – student only accommodation.

Large Student HMO – also known as **'student pods'**, which could run into hundreds of rooms.

High-spec PRS HMO – high-end look, well furnished, most rooms have en-suite bathrooms.

Co-living Concept

Co-living is often expressed through properties which are still effectively traditional HMO properties, focussed very much on a group of individuals. However, properly conceived co-living properties are a revolutionary change in the way that space can be used by communities of people.

Co-living is touted as an innovative and sociable lifestyle for generation rent, yet what's its appeal? And is it really any different from a house share?

The number of 18-35-year-olds living in house shares has doubled since 1980. With tenants in London spending on average more than a third of their monthly wage on rent, it's perhaps no surprise that innovative communal living concepts such as co-living are drawing so much interest.

Boiled down to its fundamentals, co-living may appear like an on-trend, premium spin on the traditional house share. Out are grimy kitchens and draughty bedrooms and in are designer interiors and cinema rooms. However, as the term itself hints, co-living does not simply propose a house to share. It promises a shared way of living.

For some this marketing gloss belies the reality of co-living, in which tenants rent a private room but share communal facilities, as they do in HMOs. For others, failing to distinguish between the two is to gravely misunderstand this innovative form of living that can assist in alleviating pressing social issues such as loneliness

London is home to the world's largest self-styled co-living space. The Collective Old Oak in north-west London has a staggering 550 bedrooms. The scale of such shared living complexes and the array of services they offer distinguish them from your typical HMO. Your normal flat share's facilities usually extend to kitchens, bathrooms and living rooms. Old Oak meanwhile boasts a wealth of facilities, including a gym, a cinema, and a 'library of things' – a store of useful household and DIY tools such as tape measures and hammers.

Many complexes marketed as co-living seem to be aimed at a niche higher end of the market. HMOs or 'house shares' are meanwhile usually more evenly distributed throughout it. Admittedly at the upper-end of the market – even for co-living – the Staten Island Urby in New York sounds more like a 5-star hotel than a home. It has bamboo flooring, on-site restaurants and a heated swimming pool. Yet other planned co-living spaces such as Noiascape's Red House in London are hardly offering the bare essentials. The prototype space will include yoga rooms, a library and a rooftop garden.

These large purpose-built HMOs enable tenants to share, have in-house amenities, keep housing costs down and make new social connections, in today's internet and technology age this model of housing can only grow....

Whether you think
you can or think you
can't, you're right
- Henry Ford

The Collective in Old Oak Common London & Student Pods.

Examples of how clever design and functional interiors create a feeling of space and positive atmosphere.

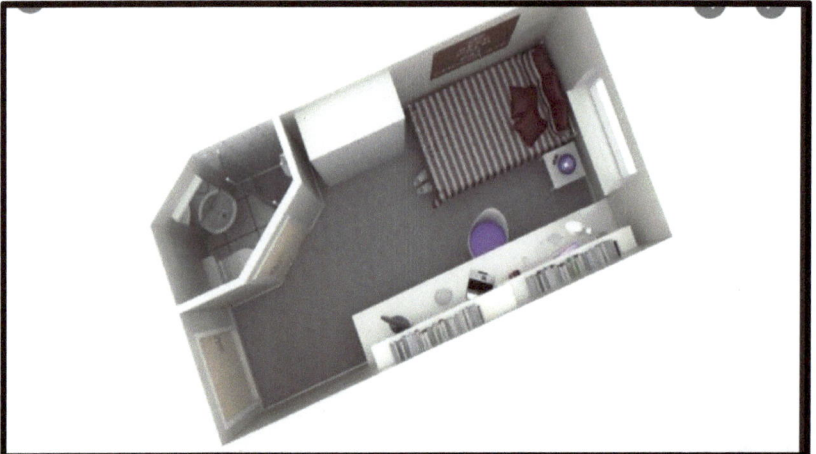

Student pod with living space, also can be termed a Studio.

Co-Living & HMOs Social and Environmental Effects

Co living allows less stress on urbanisation and helps with loneliness. Whether a large 550 room Co Living building or a 5-bedroom HMO, effectively this concept allows a lot more people to live in the same building than would otherwise in the conventional single dwelling format. This can only be beneficial to the environment, it means fewer buildings will house the same number of people, therefore less carbon footprint and effect on our environment.

Another advantage is shared spaced helps with lessening loneliness, one of the main reasons why tenants prefer to share then rent a single dwelling is that they get to make new friends. This in turn has a positive effect on the chances of stopping people going into depression, because feeling low or depressed is worsened if one lives alone.

Co-Living & Planning

Co-living has no planning class and often Hotel class is used for larger scale buildings.

Another is the following interpretation from the Mayor's Office:

Large-scale purpose-built shared living Sui Generis use developments, where of good quality and design, may have a role in meeting housing need in London if, at the neighbourhood level, the development contributes to a mixed and inclusive neighbourhood

Planning permission may be required to change the use of a building. In the current London development and planning climate, that could mean from B1 (offices) to C1 (hotel). The length of stay can impact upon the use designated for the co-living scheme. While this is a factor, it is not the only one to consider. The extent to which the individual units are self-contained and capable of occupation as standalone units is also a significant consideration. Likewise, if people are in fact occupying units as their primary residence for long periods, there is still a risk that they are occupying them as dwellings with the resultant need to have a residential use class. If the use is residential rather than hotel, the local planning authority may expect it to include an element of affordable housing, which most co-living developers and operators are keen to avoid.

HMO INVESTMENT
How to Get Involved

Typically, my HMOs are all residential. I'll buy a house, a large flat or a disused care home, with a view to transforming the property into a commercial enterprise that can generate an income.

Most HMO rentals include all bills, internet costs and cleaning of common parts of the property.

I want anyone reading this book to find out the following…

- How they can get involved in HMOs
- Financing an HMO project
- What is the main criteria for choosing location, house type, purchase price etc.
- How to manage HMOs
- And all about the pitfalls!

My aim with each project is to produce quality, tenant focused, hi-spec PRS (private rental sector) residential property, operated in a professional way and on a commercial basis.

Where possible, most of the rooms have en-suite bathrooms. There is a communal kitchen, and some with snack stations in each room, i.e. a fridge, a microwave, toaster and a kettle.

The process should always start with the correct 'Field Work'. Let's break it down into more detail…

FIELD WORK & INTERNAL REPORT

Through contacts I am made aware of towns and cities that offer HMO development opportunities, like for example Exeter (attached report at the end of the book). So, I follow-up on the best leads and I have an internal report prepared, which includes an evaluation of the specific demographics of that particular urban area. This considers...

The local area...an assessment is crucial

- Assess the specific employment sectors.
- Are jobs freely available?
- Population – is it increasing?
- Demographics is it a young or older population, as generally younger people rent HMOs.
- Is there regeneration in the area?
- Is the local council being proactive in bringing in investment?
- Is the need for employment and demand for rental properties rising?
- Are there any restrictions on conversions from single unit houses to HMO use?

The housing market...a thorough analysis is vital

- House prices – what are terrace, semi-detached and detached properties selling for in various locations in that area?
- A rigorous room rental assessment – preferably through online web portals and speaking with local HMO agents.
- Yield comparisons – i.e. the typical rents achievable for properties at the various locations identified, so we can assess the variants in the yields.
- Who are the best HMO agents?
- A report is prepared on the merits of the area for HMO investment.

Next step, I check the report. If I think the area is progressive and vibrant, then I focus on the yield and the house prices, and the areas within the city where there is greater demand and the yields are higher.

If all that works out, then I start calling the agents I have identified, to ask them about the occupancy rates, demand and supply, general landlord trends, i.e. has there been an influx of investor landlords buying up properties to convert into HMOs, which is not a positive as there could be an oversupply and depreciate rental values.

And, crucially, I check if there is an Article 4 in place anywhere in this town – this is where in certain locations within the city you cannot convert properties into HMOs, this is usually because there are too many HMO landlords already in place.

If I have satisfactory answers to all of the above, then I will choose one agent to go with, and ask them to source me properties to view.

Once initial viewings are secured, and only once they are secured, I visit the town. My system is methodical and thorough, I go step by step, and at each step I must be satisfied to move to the next, I do not want to waste valuable time on places that do not add up.

GOOD TOWNS TO INVEST

One of the main growth areas recently has been the commuter belt towns around London. These are towns, which have good access to London or other local commercial hubs via the rail transportation system. Ideally the towns should not be more than 1 hour away by train and houses should not be more than £300,000 to buy.

Some of these towns are near major airports like Bishop's Stortford, which feeds off Stanstead Airport, many airline employees live in the local HMOs and flats. This town is 57 minutes to London Liverpool Street station, so can also attract commuters.

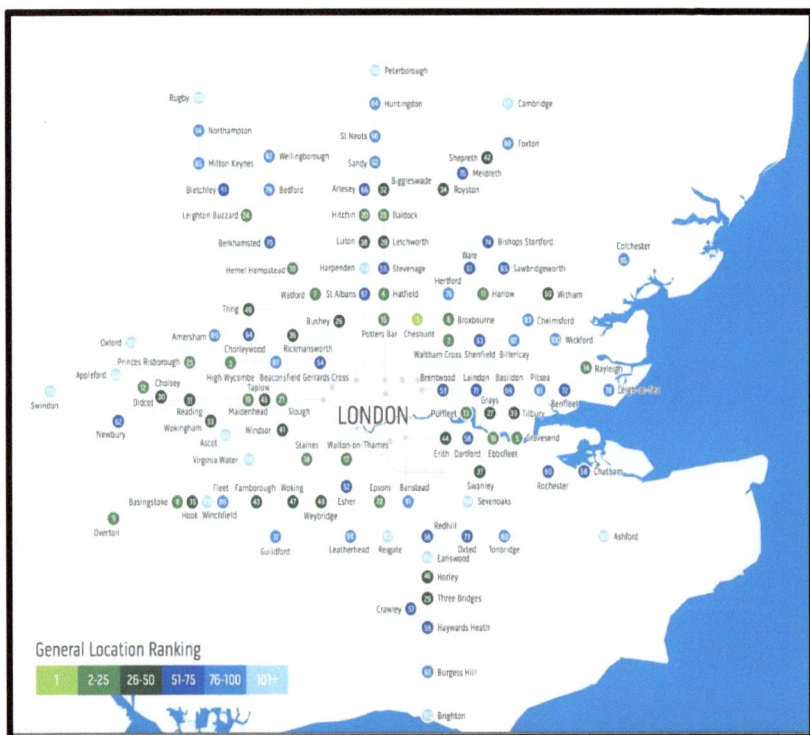

General Location Ranking

| 1 | 2-25 | 26-50 | 51-75 | 76-100 | 101+ |

Northern cities offer great returns too, for example, Manchester and Birmingham have recently had a boom in their economies.

What I have found through my research is that Northern towns offer better yields...some are as high as 15% return on investment compared to at best 10% in the South, but the capital growth is generally better in the South. In the Northern cities you can pick up properties in some areas terrace houses for £50,000- £60,000 but these are specialist localities where you need to know your tenant client base and work with good managing agents. The reason for the high yields is due to the very low capital values of the properties.

Coastal towns also offer good yields as the house prices are lower, but you need to be wary of some of these towns as they can lack local investment and cater for majority DSS tenants. With towns such as these there is absolutely nothing wrong from a human angle but from a capital growth basis and tenant end user status for my upscale PRS model it will not work. Coastal towns such as Eastbourne and Hastings work, as there is inward investment and migration coupled with pro-active local councils and PPP (private public partnership) investments.

The man who has
confidence in himself
gains the confidence
of others

- Hasidic Proverb

The Process of Assessment Begins

First, I walk the town…

- Check the side streets leading into the properties I'm viewing.
- How do the other houses look?
- Is it a deprived area or well kept?
- Are there credible people living there?
- Is the area transient?
- Is there much graffiti, for instance?
- Access to shops…supermarkets?
- I try to get a feel for positive vibes and characteristics.
- Next, I look at where the transport links are? These are key, because the people who rent these properties will want good rail or bus links and to be within walking distance to the town centre.
- Are there properties close to employment centres – business parks, factories, or warehouses? For instance, in Swindon, the properties don't need to be close to the town centre, they need to be close to the business parks.

TOP TIP

If you are investing into a town/city you are not familiar with, then it's vital to get the right advice on the criteria that is important for tenants when they are looking for accommodation. In Eastbourne the rooms should be located no more than 15 minutes' walk to town centre and mainline rail station. Whereas in Swindon which is more spaced out and has many industrial parks, the properties need to be close to these employment centres and with good bus connections. In Exeter zone 2 works well, this is just outside the centre where all the shops and the main station is located, it's walking distance, but buses are the key connectors. So, my search was for houses which were walking distance from bus stops which take you to town centre within 10-15 minutes.

What to avoid specifically

- ♦ I avoid high HMO locations and the possibility of over-supply of HMOs therefore demand will be low, and rents depressed.

- ♦ I avoid an Article 4 area – where the local authority has regulated in such a way that you cannot convert a non-HMO into an HMO.

- ♦ I avoid towns with high unemployment and where there is high outward migration.

- ♦ Where property values are too high in relation to the rental incomes, therefore yields and return on your investment will be low.

- ♦ Avoid deprived areas with social problems.

Viewing the actual properties

Once a property has been located for you by the local agents, it's important to do your vital checks.

I check the exterior to see that the property is sound, ahead of getting my surveyor's official assessment.

Ideally, I'm looking for semi-detached or detached properties. These have easier access for push bikes, etc, but I do purchase terraced property too.

Inside, I'm looking for un-modernised properties. The worst it looks aesthetically, the better. Ideally probate sales (they will be sold cheaper, as the relatives want a quick sale, for their inheritance).

If the house looks bad, then most people are put off. If it's less attractive to Joe Public, the price will be cheaper.

The layout of the property is very important. If the house is too narrow, you can't have a corridor through the middle.

TOP TIP

All my prices and evaluations are based on square feet. Meaning I divide the selling price of the house by the internal area, i.e. House sale price is £200,000, internal area is 1,500 square feet, therefore price per square feet is £133! This then is compared to other similar located properties in similar condition to give me a more accurate assessment on whether I am buying at the right price.

WHAT WORKS IN RECONFIGURING A HOUSE?

Ideally, if a house has a living room and a dining room downstairs i.e. a through lounge, then that's great. A partition is placed between the two rooms, a stud wall, this is an interior wall consisting of a frame of upright timbers to which laths and plasterboard are attached.

Usually with such an arrangement I add back to back en-suite shower rooms, meaning on either side of the stud wall, therefore allowing the same plumbing infrastructure to be used, hence cutting down on costs.

If we are having two bedrooms on the ground floor, it's vital that we have three rentable rooms on the 1st floor, to fulfil my minimum rental room criteria of 5 rooms per house.

ROOM SIZE GUIDANCE

These are guidance for HMO Licencing, but I would advise that all readers of this book check again with HMO licensing laws as they can change with time. I need a minimum habitable space of 7 square metres per room for a single occupant or 11.5 square metres for two co-habiting as a couple (that's the law, regulation). If I've got 10 square metres for each room, then 3 square metres can be used for en-suite bathrooms.

KITCHEN FACILITIES, LOUNGE & ROOM SIZES

Usually I arrange the lounge/living space off the kitchen, this flows better and often tenants like to congregate and meet in the kitchen, plus saves on space.

Kitchens are normally basic white kitchen cabinets with wooden worktops and if possible nice knobs, with simple but colour coordinated splash backs. Here it's important to give some **wow!** factor with the colours rather than any upscale brand. I often buy from Howden's Trade kitchens, their goods are well priced and discounted for tradesmen, so your builder can use their discount and pass on the saving to you.

You will need to provide a TV in the living room or kitchen. All white goods need to be supplied, a double fridge to accommodate so many tenants, integrated washer/dryer as often if tenants do not have a dryer, they hang their washed clothing in their rooms or common areas, which is unsightly and can cause mould from the damp. I also provide a dishwasher, a cooker minimum 5/6 ring (I prefer electric, it's safer in my opinion) or two cookers if your HMO is more than 8 rooms, plus an oven or two with larger HMOs.

The HMO licensing guidance for a kitchen up to 5 persons is 5.5 square metres. Lounge/Living room 1-3 people is 5.5 square metre, and 4-6 people is 11 square metres.

A Selection of photos from my portfolio of HMO Developments

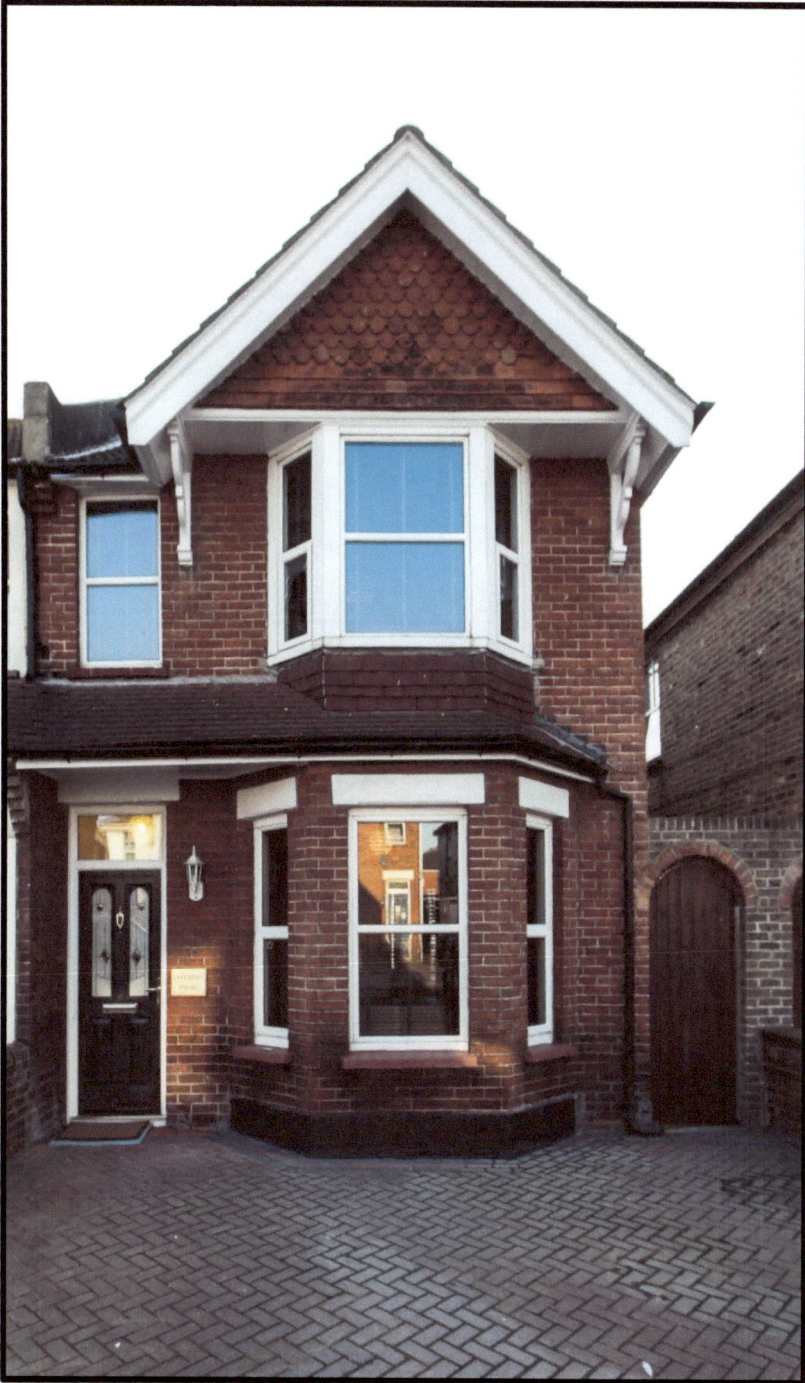

Examples of layouts.

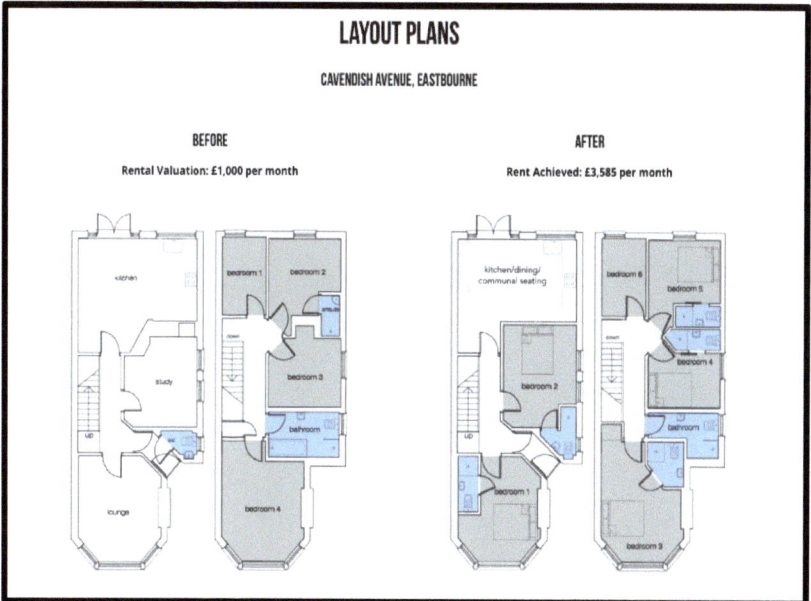

LAYOUT PLANS

CAVENDISH AVENUE, EASTBOURNE

BEFORE
Rental Valuation: £1,000 per month

AFTER
Rent Achieved: £3,585 per month

OXFORD ROAD, SWINDON

BEFORE
Rental Valuation: £1,000 per month

AFTER
Rent Achieved: £3,250 per month

The only limit to our
realisation of tomorrow
will be our doubts of today

- Franklin D. Roosevelt

Flow of The House

The flow of the house is very important when it's converted into an HMO, as all tenants need access to the common areas without intruding on one another's private space, namely their rented room. Access means to the main door, rear garden, common kitchen, common bathroom and common living area.

Otherwise the house needs to be wide enough to create access to the common area/kitchen for everyone.

Note - a lot of small or narrow houses don't work as HMOs, so it makes the research even more important...and shows how crucial it is to get a good local strategic partner/agent, because they will know every street in the locality.

It helps if there's a conservatory at the back of the property (or option to build one) for extra living or communal space.

Note - with a house or garden flat, some people will have access to the garden from their rooms, but all must have access to the garden through a corridor or common area.

TOP TIPS

Maximising your box room

If a house has three bedrooms upstairs (one a box room) and a bathroom, I convert the box room into an en-suite for the adjacent bedroom, and the main bathroom becomes an off-suite to the other. However, in such instances the house must have the potential to reconfigure the ground floor into 3 rentable rooms to fulfil the minimum 5 rental room criteria.

Adaptive Spaces and Break Out Areas

Fully equipped cafe kitchens provide great spaces to eat meals and socialise together. Lounge areas, which usually flow from the kitchen space should be adaptive so that they can be used as dining space or areas to sit and read a book, or to meet and chat with other tenants.

Break out areas are where you can utilise the hallway (if large enough) as secondary quiet areas where tenants can sit alone to contemplate their day or week ahead.

The following photographs are from **HMO** developments in Hove by another progressive developer, interior features have created a hip shabby-chic look.

TOP TIPS

Converting Garages

Garages that are attached to the side of the house can be converted with planning permission into habitable space or another bedroom. To convert into a bedroom there must be a window created (planning permission needed).

Rear Extensions & Loft Conversions

To increase the size of your house, one can add a rear extension, permission can be granted by using permitted development rights the following guidelines are applicable. Single storey rear extension must not extend beyond the rear of the original house by more than 3 metres to attached house or by 4 metres if a detached house.

It's vital with HMO development that the area created can add extra space internally for a further 'let-able' room, as you do not want to create extra internal space for the sake of making the house larger. The spend must go towards creating greater rental income.

The main rules for extensions to houses:

- No more than half the area of land around the original house should be covered by additions or other buildings.
- No extension will project forward of the principal elevation or side elevation fronting a highway (which means that the new extension should not go beyond the front or side of the original house that leads on to the street).
- No extension is to be higher than the highest part of the roof.
- Single-storey rear extensions must not extend beyond the rear wall of the original house by more than 3m if an attached house or by 4m if a detached house. However, the limit is increased to 6m if an attached house and 8m if a detached house until 30 May 2019. These increased limits are subject to providing the local authority with prior notification of the work. A neighbour consultation scheme will take place and if objections are received, the proposal might not be allowed.
- Maximum height of a single-storey rear extension of 4m.
- Extensions of more than one storey must not extend beyond the rear wall of the original house by more than 3m.
- Side extensions to be single storey with a maximum height of 4m and width of no more than half that of the original house.
- Two-storey extensions to be no closer than 7m to rear boundary.
- Roof pitch of extensions higher than one storey to match existing house.
- Materials to be similar in appearance to the existing house.
- No verandas, balconies or raised platforms.

TOP TIPS

Oversized Skylights

If a loft is going to be converted it is important that you add skylights.

You do not normally need to apply for planning permission to re-roof your house or to insert roof lights or skylights as the permitted development rules allow for roof alterations subject to the following limits and conditions. Any alteration to project no more than 150 millimetres from the existing roof plane. The bigger the skylight the better from an aesthetic point of view, the room will look larger.

Extending a flat

The planning rules for flats and maisonettes are stricter than for houses. To add an extension to your flat, you will have to apply for planning permission. Similarly, if you're planning to convert the loft in a top-floor flat, the rules are a bit woolly and you will need to check with your local planning authority.

You may not need it if alterations are just internal, but it will be required if you want to extend or alter the roof space. You will also need to check whether you own the roof space. If you are a leaseholder, the freeholder is likely to charge a fee for this.

Expect to pay £1,480 a square metre for a 20 square metre loft conversion, which works out at £29,600. This is for a plaster finished shell with dormer and Velux windows and includes construction costs.

Loft conversions are again a very good way of increasing the internal rentable space for your property, there are head height restrictions. Minimum room sizes also apply as well as a minimum floor to ceiling height of 2.3m for at least 75% of the gross internal area.

A loft conversion for your house is considered to be permitted development, not requiring an application for planning permission, subject to the following conditions:

- A volume allowance of 40 cubic metres additional roof space for terraced houses.

- A volume allowance of 50 cubic metres additional roof space for detached and semi-detached houses.

- No extension beyond the plane of the existing roof slope of the principal elevation that fronts the highway.

- No extension to be higher than the highest part of the roof.

- Materials to be similar in appearance to the existing house.

- No verandas, balconies or raised platforms.

- Side-facing windows to be obscure-glazed; any opening to be 1.7m above the floor.

- Roof extensions not to be permitted development in designated areas.

- Roof extensions, apart from hip to gable ones, to be set back, as far as practicable, at least 20cm from the original eaves.

- The roof enlargement cannot overhang the outer face of the wall of the original house.

In all conversions and build extensions you are required to inform the Local Authority Building Regulations Department. The building inspector will inspect that the works have been completed according to local authority build regulations and upon completion will provide a build completion certificate.

Basement Dig-Outs

There are real benefits from a basement dig out conversion. These include an increase in floor area without an increase in the size of the footprint of a building or a significant impact on the size of the garden.

As earlier covered in "High-End Property Developing" section, I completed a development project where I dug out a 9-metre-deep basement. This created a double storey living space below ground, at project completion Ensor Mews in South Kensington become a 4-storey building.

One important point is that it gets more expensive the further down you go, this is particularly so for deeper basement excavations that pass the water table. This will mean the installation of a water-proof membrane and even a water pump. Please note with HMO developments in lower-end priced properties, the higher basement build costs may not out-way the actual returns, so keep to accurate appraisals for returns on funds invested.

Turning an existing cellar into habitable space by tanking and insulating the walls will cost circa £125 - £165 per square foot – around the same as a loft conversion. Factors that will increase costs include the need to move services, underpinning, and lowering the floor level to increase ceiling height.

Constructing a brand-new basement under an existing house and underpinning the walls will cost £185 to £260 per square foot for a shell finish. These costs will increase if there is the need for any party wall agreements with neighbours whose boundary walls will be affected, or if there are difficult ground conditions or poor access to the site for the work to be completed.

Installing a light well or new external access door will cost £5,000 to £9,000 each.

You will also have to factor in additional costs for finishes, flooring, painting & decorating and any additional costs for bathroom or kitchen. In Central London the complete job can cost you up to £450 per square foot for upscale high spec finished properties.

Converting an existing residential cellar or basement into a living space is in most cases unlikely to require planning permission as long as it is not a separate unit or unless the usage is significantly changed or a light well is added, which alters the external appearance of the property.

Excavating to create a new basement involves major works. A new separate unit of accommodation alters the external appearance of the house, such as adding a light well will require planning permission. If you live in a listed building you are likely to need consent for internal or external work. Some basements extend into the garden; therefore, a basement can literally cover the whole footprint of the house and most of the garden.

Loft conversion, rear / side extension and basement conversion can potentially increase the gross internal area by up to 70%". However, it is of paramount importance that the actual cost of increasing the floor space is in line with increases in net revenue from the rental income.

TOP TIPS

Certificate of Lawfulness

This is when you are making a planning application, you confirm in your application that an existing structure or use has been in situ within Article 83A Certificate of Lawfulness of Existing Use or Development. Therefore, you are requesting to bring this into lawful permission via the planning application.

Do what you can
with all you have,
wherever you are

\- Theodore Roosevelt

High Spec and Quality Finishes

My aim is to create a quality homely feel to the HMO property, so prospective tenants are instantly attracted to it from the moment they walk in.

High spec and quality finishes need not cost so much. Just take care with choosing eye catching furniture and the right colour schemes. Plenty of pictures and homely messages create a warm environment for tenants.

I use an interior designer who charges a fee for their services. However, people who have the time can quite easily facilitate this themselves. Most items are available online. Ikea is a good place to find the right merchandise. You can also go and visit large residential projects where they have show flats/houses. You can take photographs and pick up some excellent ideas created by professional interior designers. All bedrooms should come with a double bed (most often 4ft 6ins), a bed side cabinet, wardrobes, a chest of drawers, side lamp, and I normally have fixed pendant from the ceiling for main room light fitting.

Some of the larger rooms are provided with 'snack stations'. This is often the provision of a fridge, microwave, toaster and kettle. This adds value and you can charge a higher rental for these rooms and they also rent out quicker.

Fixtures and fittings
- I fit thick quality carpets on the staircases, hallways, living areas and bedrooms. Visually, this gives a feeling of comfort and homeliness. Secondly and most importantly it cuts down on the noise from the multiple occupants, particularly ladies walking around in high heels on hard surfaces which can create a lot of noise. Bathrooms and kitchen floors are all surfaced with commercial heavy-duty vinyl, which is quick to install and cost effective.

- For the walls within the shower cubicle in the bathrooms I use Geo panels rather than tiles which have lower maintenance costs, I don't need to re-grout in the future and avoids water penetration as there are no gaps.
- All bedrooms and kitchen/living areas are fitted with internet port sockets so that laptops or games console can be plugged in directly.
- All rooms have Venetian slate blinds, giving an upscale feel, while they are low on maintenance and durable.
- A garden should also be low maintenance with some greenery, and ideally not too many flowers. I often use shingle to cover hard surfaces, it's cheap and quick to lay and looks good with minimal maintenance. The aim of the exercise is to keep on-going upkeep costs down. You don't want to be spending a lot of money on gardener pruning and replacing dead flowers because tenants have not looked after them. I always provide garden furniture as part of the attraction in living in an HMO house is the outside space.

Examples of how quality carpet covering creates a luxuriant homely feel.

COLOUR SCHEME

I keep to light earthy colours for the interior walls. I have used cornflour white on many occasions throughout the house and steppingstone white on the feature wall in the bedrooms. I have incorporated interior themes such as the seaside, whereby the colours are differing shades of blue with coordinating pictures and accessories. Ceilings are always white.

CUTLERY, CROCKERY AND COOKING UTENSILS

All my HMOs and even single let dwellings (regular flats) are provided with a stock of cutlery, crockery, pots and pans. As these are furnished lets, the tenants do expect them to be fully kitted out but do keep to cheap brands and expect breakages. The breakages are covered by the tenant's deposits.

FIRE SECURITY & REGULATIONS

It's imperative to be within the law when it comes to fire security. There are strict regulations to be adhered to. Please see some of these below:

FIRE EXTINGUISHERS

In HMOs simple multi-purpose extinguishers are required on each floor in the common parts. Fire extinguishers should be maintained annually to BS 5306-3. This needs to be done by fire extinguisher service engineers, unless service-free extinguishers are deployed.

RISK ASSESMENT

Under the Housing Act 2004 and the Regulatory Reform (Fire Safety) Order 2005 HMOs are required to undertake fire risk assessments. Landlords should note that they are not expected to train tenants in fire safety, but that this is merely a document to outline where the hazards lie and how they can be avoided.

FIRE DOORS

HMO Fire Door Regulations. Fire doors are an essential feature of HMO fire safety regulations. The rule is that, as a landlord, you need to make sure that all escape routes from the property are protected. We also install a fire door in the communal lounge.

SMOKE DETECTORS

Tenants cannot remove the smoke detectors and must ensure that batteries are regularly replaced. A landlord has limited ability to ensure working smoke detectors in a rental property if the tenant or the tenant's guests do not take responsibility for proper maintenance and upkeep.

FIRE ALARMS

For many years NFPA 72, National Fire Alarm and Signalling Code, has required as a minimum that smoke alarms be installed inside every sleep room (even for existing homes). In addition, smoke alarms are required outside each sleeping area and on every level of the home. (Additional smoke alarms are required for larger homes).

HMO FLATS

I have HMO flats within my portfolio, these also work financially. For example, I purchased a block of four flats in Eastbourne, which was a repossession from the bank. The property was reconfigured to add an extra bedroom per dwelling while retaining the existing separated four residential units. This means each flat has three letting rooms. Additional bedrooms were created in the existing living rooms, in some cases adding a stud wall. Kitchen counter-tops, new carpets, painting and decorating formed the enhancement of the property, plus I added the magic of attractive eye-catching furnishings and accessories. Through this development process I created four long residential leases. If needed I can in the future sell each unit separately.

No HMO licence was needed. The result of the reconfiguration/refurbishment increased gross rent from £3,000 per month to £5,800 per month for the four flats.

Develop an 'Attitude Of Gratitude'. Say thank you to everyone you meet for everything they do for you

- Brian Tracy

Block of Flats - HMO Development

Pre & Post Development Plans

Flat 1 - Rear- Ground & 1st Floor Duplex House
Flat 2 - Ground Floor Unit
Flat 3 - First Floor Unit
Flat 4 - Second Floor Unit

Pre-Refurbishment/Reconfiguration

Flat 1 - Rear - Ground & 1st Floor Duplex House
Flat 2 - Ground Floor Unit
Flat 3 - First Floor Unit
Flat 4 - Second Floor Unit

Post-Refurbishment/Reconfiguration

Post-Development Layout – number of letting rooms increased by 50%.

'Be Proud of What You Own'
MAINTAINING PROPERTIES IN GOOD ORDER

I ensure that all maintenance and repairs are carried out within 24 hours of any calls from tenants in properties that I manage personally. This same professional principle I adhere to when replying to the managing agents' requests. Responding quickly with decisions is vital.

It's important to know good plumbers, electricians and general handymen. In each of the towns and cities I do business in I have created a network of credible professionals, who I rely on to do any repairs and maintenance at my properties.

If you want respect from tenants, you need to respect them and their requests for a quick response in repairing anything that goes wrong in the property they rent.

As a responsible landlord I always keep up maintenance, meaning the properties are painted and decorated every 18-24 months, boilers serviced annually, bed mattresses changed regularly when springs are about to go, furniture changed once it starts looking tired and old. Ultimately, you are not spending on the tenant, you are spending on your property. You own it and you should be proud of what you own!

PICKING THE RIGHT BUILDERS

This is the third key decision you need to make after the most important ones, which is the property purchase and the design scheme.

There are many types of build companies and teams, and some larger firms will not be interested in working on a smaller five-bedroom HMO property, because their operating costs will be too high. The smaller credible build teams are usually booked up months in advance, therefore it is very important to book and agree the refurbishment well in advance once you know your purchase is advancing.

I deal with various build companies, some are larger for the bigger development projects, others are three man build teams. I try and keep with the builders I know, or I go through recommendation. If the company is new to me, I meet the owner and the members of staff. I visit the building sites they are working on, get client references and even professional accountant and bank references. It's key to do your homework on any building firm before you engage them.

My build work agreements are all inclusive, including both labour and materials. On occasion I have purchased the materials myself, but that can be time consuming, plus builders usually get trade discounts therefore lowering the material costs and they can pass this on to you the client.

With smaller HMO development projects, I always work with a written estimate and scope of works. For large build jobs I and the contractor enter a detailed JTC contract. JCT contracts facilitate the process of delivering a building project. In simple terms they set out the responsibilities of all the parties within the process and their obligations to each other. In this way it is then clear what work needs to be done, who is doing it, and what is the construction timescale, any late penalty clauses, start date and total cost with a breakdown.

I manage the smaller projects myself, but with larger developments I have an architect project managing with my oversight and regular site visits. Larger more complicated builds need working drawings, which my architect prepares prior to an estimate of costs being given and these drawings are used during the build process.

One of the key reasons a builder falls out with a client is because of payments. It is imperative that if the works are completed to your satisfaction you must pay the contractor on time at every stage payment or inform them otherwise and the reason why.

This is something I have always done. I have never missed a payment, except if I am not satisfied with the work and then I do not pay and tell the contractor I will see him in court. If the builder has completed extra work or made changes which have taken up more of his time and these changes were from my instructions, then I have to pay extra. I do not argue and waste valuable time and lose respect over trying to save money this way. It does not work. If you have the respect of the contractor, the job will go smoothly, on budget and finish on time.

BUILD COSTS

I normally work out build costs on a per square foot basis (psf). This is dependent on the type of build, i.e. whether it is a new build, a conversion, office to residential, rear extension, basement build, inner city build or makeover. The quality of the specifications and materials will ultimately have a bearing on the total build cost and costs per square foot.

Let's take a house which is 1,500 square feet in size (GIA – gross internal area) and the total labour and material build cost is £100,000. This means the build cost is £67 per square foot (psf). I have paid from £40 psf for small refurbishment build jobs to £300 psf for luxury high end new builds and everything else in between. Inner London basement dig out and build jobs costs including all finishes are in the region of £400 psf.

Therefore, when I appraise a potential project, I can work the approximate build costs from multiplying the GIA and the build cost psf I deem it needs. If the project includes external plot works, I use a GEA (gross external area).

BUILDER PAYMENT SCHEDULE

I pay for the building works on my developments with smaller but regular payments, ideally weekly or bi-weekly for small projects of up to a £60,000-£70,000 build cost. The reason for smaller payments is two-fold. It works better for the contractor to have regular payments, helping their cash flow. Secondly, I personally have less risk, because if the contractor goes out of business or absconds from the site you have less to recover and more of the build has been completed within what has been spent.

With larger projects, the payments are monthly, where the contractor issues an invoice, which is then passed to a quantity surveyor (QS) who then visits the site and confirms what materials have been used

119

and what work has been done. . Usually with larger development sites the bank is funding the build and the QS represents the bank, the cost is paid by the developer.

Prior to starting any development, the build cost should be agreed, and the contractor should also provide a schedule of payments.

HMO LICENSING

All my HMO properties are licenced, except the HMO flats as these do not need a licence.

To clarify again, a house in multiple occupation (HMO) is a property rented out by at least 3 people who are not from 1 'household' (for example a family) but share facilities like the bathroom and kitchen. It's sometimes called a 'house share'.

Regulations laid in Parliament Mandatory HMO Licensing came into force from 1st October 2018.

You must have a licence if you're renting out a large HMO in England or Wales. Your property is defined as a large HMO if all of the following apply:

- it is rented to 5 or more people who form more than 1 household
- some or all tenants share toilet, bathroom or kitchen facilities
- at least 1 tenant pays rent (or their employer pays it for them)

Even if your property is smaller and rented to fewer people, you may still need a licence depending on the area. Check with your council.

Restrictions

- A licence is valid for a maximum of 5 years.
- You must renew your licence before it runs out.
- You need a separate licence for each HMO you run.

Conditions

You must make sure:

- the house is suitable for the number of occupants (this depends on its size and facilities)
- the manager of the house - you or an agent - is considered to be 'fit and proper', for example they have no criminal record or breach of landlord laws or code of practice

You must also:

- send the council an updated gas safety certificate every year
- install and maintain smoke alarms
- provide safety certificates for all electrical appliances when requested

The council may add other conditions to your licence, for example improving the standard of your facilities. They will let you know when you apply.

HIGH SPEED INTERNET AND CLEANING

In all my properties I provide high speed internet and all rooms have internet port sockets.

All common parts, kitchen, common bathrooms, hallways, need weekly cleaning, usually for a typical 5-bedroom house 3 hours of cleaning should suffice.

Fake it until you make it!
Act as if you had all the
confidence you require until
it becomes your reality

- Brian Tracy

Bank Finance

Bank finance is key to making a success in the property sector, and this is especially so for HMO properties. The aim is to use the bank's money to make money for yourself. But how, you may ask? I have given examples below showing, where you borrow from the bank at a cost of 4% in interest per annum, and the net income from the total investment is 10% per annum minus finance costs. You can see that the more you borrow and less you use of your own capital, will have an effect where your returns will be higher on your capital deployed. Conversely and effectively, your money is working harder for you when you borrow more. This is the case with low interest rates, it will be the opposite if interest rates start going up past the equilibrium point!

Below are examples where income is generating @ 10% gross on the value of the investment (property purchase value & all build & development costs). ** operating costs not included in these examples.

EXAMPLE 1 – Loan 50 % of Total Investment

Total Cost	£100,000
Borrowed 50%	£50,000
Own capital 50%	£50,000
Income @ 10% of Investment	£10,000
Cost of 50% loan @ 4% Interest per annum	£2,000
Net Income after Interest	£8,000
Return on your capital	**16%**

EXAMPLE 2 – Loan 75 % of Total Investment

Total Cost	£100,000
Borrowed 75%	£75,000
Own capital 25%	£25,000
Income @ 10% of Investment	£10,000
Cost of 75% loan @ 4% interest per annum	£3,000
Net Income after Interest	£7,000
Return on your capital	**28%**

EXAMPLE 3 – Loan 90 % of Total Investment

Total Cost	£100,000
Borrowed 90%	£90,000
Own capital 10%	£10,000
Income @ 10% of Investment	£10,000
Cost of 90% loan @ 4% interest per annum	£3,600
Net Income after Interest	£6,400
Return on your capital	**64%**

EXAMPLE 4 – Loan 100% of Total Investment NO MONEY DOWN

Total Cost	£100,000
Income @ 10% of Investment	£10,000
Borrowed 100% @ 4% interest per annum	£4,000
Net Income after Interest	£6,000

Warning It is very unlikely that any bank will lend 100% of the total investment (purchase, refurbishment and all other costs). It is very risky because if the interest rate goes above 10% the investment will start making a loss!!

TYPES OF FINANCE

The UK has a very sophisticated financial sector with a myriad of lending institutions offering many types of loans, which are dependent on the reason for the loan. Below are the types of loans that are available.

MORTGAGE

This is available for borrowers who seek a loan for purchasing their own place of residence, this loan is based not only on the value of the property but the income of the borrower. A mortgage must not be used for any commercial property purchases. The size of your income dictates the amount of loan you can borrow.

BUY TO LET LOAN

With a growth in the past decade of investors, particularly smaller investors putting their savings into property, the market for specific rental property purchase loans, has also grown. These are called BTL (Buy to Let) loans. There are many lenders offering BTL loans, some as low as 1.7% interest per annum for two-year fixed periods on low Loan to Values (LTV) i.e. 60%. The criteria for these loans are firstly the market value of the property being purchased, plus most importantly the market value of the monthly/annual rental income. Most investors take out a BTL loan on an 'Interest only' basis, meaning you are never paying the capital off, therefore keeping the monthly payments low. Generally, lenders assess the monthly income to cover the actual interest payments by 125-150%, meaning for example if you are paying £1,000 per month interest then the rental income should be at least £1,250 - £1,500, However, it's important to check as the coverage can be even higher, and this can be stress-tested, whereby a higher interest rate is used in the unforeseen circumstances that rates go up. The lender will also need the purchaser to have their own income. This is a fall-back position in case the property is not rented throughout the year, However, unlike a mortgage, the loan is not based on the borrower's personal income.

Some BTL loans go up to 85% of the property purchase, but on such higher Loan to Values the interest rates go up to circa 5%-6% per annum and so do the arrangement fees increase.

COMMERCIAL INVESTMENT LOANS

A commercial investment loan is for block purchases. This is where an investor is buying more than one unit, i.e. 3 flats in one building, each with long leases, with a share of freehold but owned by the same buyer. This type of purchase is a little more complicated. The interest rates and fees can both be higher than a straight forward single unit BTL loan, hence more paperwork and 'legal' are needed.

PROPERTY DEVELOPMENT LOANS

These types of loans are only available to investors who have experience developing property. This is a model where you buy a plot or a building, either to demolish, convert, extend or construct a new build. The lender will fund 50-60% of the purchase price and 100% of the all development costs i.e. build cost, planning fees, architects, structural engineers etc. All interest is rolled up, meaning there are no monthly loan payments and arrangement fees are added to the loan too. Everything is paid at the end of the loan period when the development is completed and sold. This is called a 'balloon payment' in banking jargon.

A property development loan can go up to a value of 85% (including interest roll up and fees) of the total costs of the project. Currently interest rates usually vary between 5% – 9% per annum, with arrangement fees between 1.5% – 3%.

BRIDGE LOANS

A bridge loan is a type of short-term loan typically taken out for a period of 2 weeks to 3 years pending the arrangement of larger or longer-term financing.

This is interim financing for an individual or business until permanent financing or the next stage of financing is obtained. Money from the new financing is generally used to "take out" (i.e. to pay back) the bridge loan, as well as other capitalisation needs.

Bridge loans are typically more expensive than conventional financing, to compensate for the additional risk. Bridge loans typically have a higher interest rates, points (points are essentially fees, 1-point equals 1% of loan amount), and other costs that are amortized over a shorter period, and various fees and other "sweeteners" (such as equity participation by the lender in some loans).

Usually with Bridge Loans, there are fewer questions asked, and they are not dependent on income derived from the property. The most important criteria is the value of the asset, and how you will pay back the loan. Bridge loans tend to be up to 70-75% loan to value, with interest rates in the 7% - 10% range.

HMO LOANS

This is a specific loan that is only offered by some lenders to experienced HMO owner/operators.

This is a Buy to Let loan based on the income generated by an existing operational HMO. The value of the property is not just open market but has a commercial value, meaning the property has a higher value because it is a high yielding licensed HMO unit. The valuation can be 25-50% higher than a similar non-HMO property on the same street in the same condition.

It does matter what the yield is, therefore generally the higher the yield the higher the value difference between two properties sitting side by side, one HMO and the other a regular single dwelling.

Therefore, once a property is purchased converted and licensed into an HMO, and you have at least 6-12 months HMO operating experience, you can refinance with an HMO loan at a higher revaluation and take out a chunk of your money, which will mean your return on your capital will increase dramatically. I have given examples in this book.

BANK ARRANGEMENT AND BROKER FEES

As explained previously there are many types of loans depending on the reason why you are borrowing. The bank makes money from the interest it charges, which can vary dependent on the type of loan and the risk involved. The bigger the loan in relation to the asset value (the property) the higher the interest rate, which in today's market this can be as high as 10% for a 1st charge Bridge loan, compared to being as low as 1.5% for a residential amortised mortgage with a low loan to value.

There are other charges the borrower has to be aware of, such as arrangement fees. This is another form of income the bank makes from lending, it is a one-off payment and reflects a fixed percentage of the loan facility, most often it varies from 0.75% to 3% of the total loan amount. There is no common ground on what is charged, it again depends why the arrangement fee is being charged. With short term loans such as Bridge funding the arrangement fees are high because the loan is out for a short period therefore the bank needs to work its money harder. With a long-term residential loan repaid on a capital and interest term basis, the loans are lower risk with often penalty fees applicable if it is paid off or refinanced within the first few years, therefore the arrangement fees are nominal sums if at all.

I use finance brokers to assist with finding the right funding option. The broker looks through all the banks offering various finance deals and presents to me a short list of potentials. After deciding which bank to go with the broker will approach the bank on my behalf and get an in principle yes with indicative terms. If I am happy to proceed the broker will then make a direct application to the bank, and at this stage some brokers charge a fee for their services. Usually brokers make their fees from the lender, but some charge the client too, but everything is transparent, and you will know how much the broker is making from your loan.

The reason I use a broker is because they are able to scrutinise all the lenders, get the best deal for me and then package my application so that my loan request is successful.

Things work out best
for those who make the
best of how things work out
- John Wooden

The Buying Process

If any of the houses I view are right for me, I put in a formal offer. How to structure an offer to show you are serious.

♦ Show proof of funds...a bank statement showing that you have capital and a letter of support from your bank or finance broker.

♦ Confirm your lawyer details and even copy them into you're correspondence. (Now, the agent is taking you seriously)

♦ Contact your broker, the broker prepares everything to secure a loan, so you don't use all your capital.

♦ The buying process, via the financing process, begins.

Purchase Completion Process - Finance

I notify the agent that I may be using cash...or cash and a bridge loan. My architect is primed in case there are any planning changes. But the architect is not employed until I've actually exchanged on the property.

Then once I have exchanged (usually 10% down but can be 5% for larger purchases) and if there is a planning application needed, I try and delay the completion so the 90 - 95% balance is paid as late as possible. The completion can be in some instances three to four months from date of exchange. Some sellers are willing to even wait longer if they know a sale is going to go through with the 10% deposit down. However, often the purchase is part of a chain and even if the seller has agreed it is conditional on the seller of the property they are buying agreeing too.

By delaying the completion of the purchase, you are delaying borrowing the money, and save on the interest.

Once property purchase is completed, I use "The 3 Month Rule".

For 5-6 room HMO development projects my aim is that from the time of purchase, the property should have been refurbished, furnished and let out within 3 months!!

Funding the Purchase

As I mentioned I use my own capital and bank finance. Usually for the purchase the bank finance would be a Bridge Loan, this can fund up to circa 70-75% of the purchase price, the remaining 25-30% and all refurbishment and other costs I pay with my own capital.

EXAMPLE

Property Purchase	£300,000
Build works, furniture, legal fees etc	£70,000
Total Investment	**£370,000**

Funding

Bridge Funding @ 70% of purchase price	£210,000
Buyer capital funding @ 30% of purchase price	£90,000
Buyer capital funding for build works, furniture etc	£70,000

Therefore, the buyer has to invest £90,000 for purchase plus £70,000 for development costs, a total of £160,000 of their own capital.

'THE POWER OF LEVERAGE'

Re-financing once the property is set up as an HMO. Once the property is converted and is an operational HMO, I go to an HMO specialist lender and seek to refinance the property, I can do this immediately, but currently first time HMO operators will need to wait 6 – 12 months to show a track record. Now that I have a high-income generating HMO, I can request a higher valuation for my property. Let's take my example below of a 35% higher revaluation for the above property purchased for £300,000.
EXAMPLE

Property originally purchased	£300,000
35% increase in value post refurbishment	£105,000
New valuation	**£405,000**

I approach the new HMO lender with a new property valuation of £405,000. My application will be for an 80% loan to new valuation. Please see below the example.

EXAMPLE

New HMO property value	£405,000
Refinance loan @ 80% of Value	£324,000
Original Bridge Loan	**£210,000**

After refinancing with the HMO loan and paying off the Bridge Loan I can take out the surplus cash of £114,000.

Summary

Original capital I invested	£160,000
Refinancing money taken out	£114,000
Capital remaining in investment	**£46,000**

Cash flow from Refinanced HMO

Let's take an example of an operational HMO, which is gross yielding 10%. This means the actual income before operational costs and finance costs. This is 10% of the total investment (purchase, build and other related costs).

EXAMPLE

Total costs (purchase & build)	£370,000
Income @ 10% of total investment/costs	£37,000
Less operational costs, managing agents, utilities, council tax etc @ 30% of income	£11,100
Net income before bank finance payments	£25,900
Deduct Bank finance interest @ 4% of loan	**£12,960**
Net Income after finance payments	£12,940
Capital left in the property after Refinancing	£46,000
Return on your remaining capital invested	**28%**

You can see the 'Power of Leverage', your £46,000 is earning you £12,940. which is 28% per annum. If that same money was left in the bank it would have earned £230 at current bank deposit rates of circa 0.5%. However, with this investment model you are earning 56 times more!

Interest Only Loans

I focus on refinancing with an 'interest only' loan. The reason for this is that repayments are substantially lower. It gives a far higher return on the equity remaining in the property. The aim of the exercise is to get your money working hard for you.

The proviso is that your debt never goes down. However, over a period of years the value of the property should go up and therefore the loan to actual value will decrease and your equity increase. The second positive is that the high net cashflow will mean the investor will get their remaining capital back within a short period of time, most often in today's market within four to five years.

FINANCIALS – HMO Investing with High Returns

I have below given 3 financial examples with spreadsheets. **1)** pure cash investment and no debt. **2)** cash investment then refinance with

HMO loan. **3)** cash plus bridge loan to purchase and refinancing with HMO loan.

Note: for all 3 financial spreadsheets the 8% rental management fee includes voids.

Pure Cash Investment No Debt

HMO Property Development Financials - No Debt	
Purchase Price (including stamp duty)	£300,000
Valuation Fee	£1,000
Legal Fees for Property Purchase	£1,500
Refurbishment Costs	£50,000
Furniture, white Goods & accessories	£10,000
Agent sourcing Fees	£2,500
Architect & Planning/building regs fees	£2,500
Misc. & Unexpected Expenses	£2,500
Total Costs	**£370,000**
Rental Income	
Annual Income	£37,200
Rental Monthly	£3,100
Voids @ 5%	£155
Lettings Fee @ 8% of rental income	£236
Utilities (gas/electric/water) & council tax	£375
Accountancy Fees	£60
Internet	£50
Cleaning	£50
Building Insurance	£30
Total Costs	£956
Operating costs as percentage of gross rental income	30.8%
Gross yield on total Investment	**10%**
Net Income (before tax)	**£2,144**

Return on Capital	7%

Cash Investment Then Refinance with HMO Loan

HMO Property Development Financials - Refinance HMO LOAN	
Purchase Price (including stamp duty)	£300,000
Valuation Fee	£1,000
Legal Fees for Property Purchase	£1,500
Refurbishment Costs	£50,000
Furniture, white Goods & accessories	£10,000
Agent sourcing Fees	£2,500
Architect & Planning/building regs fees	£2,500
Misc. & unexpected Expenses	£2,500
HMO Loan arrangement fees @ 2% of loan value	£6,480
Total Costs	£376,480
HMO valuation @ 35% higher value	£405,000
HMO Loan to New Valuation @ 80%	£324,000
Capital remaining in investment post HMO refinancing	**£52,480**
Rental Income	
Annual Income	£37,200
Rental Monthly	£3,100
Loan repayments @ 4% per annum interest	£1,080
Voids @ 5%	£155
Lettings Fee @ 8% of rental income	£236
Utilities (gas/electric/water) & council tax	£375
Accountancy Fees	£60

Internet	£50
Cleaning	£50
Building Insurance	£30
Total Costs	£2,036
Operating costs & debt repayments as percentage of gross rental income	65.7%
Gross yield on total Investment	**9.9%**
Net Income (before tax)	**£1,064**
Return on remaining capital	**24%**

Cash Plus Bridge Loan to Purchase and Refinancing with HMO Loan

HMO Property Development Financials - Bridging & HMO LOAN	
Purchase Price (including stamp duty)	£300,000
Valuation Fee	£1,000
Legal Fees for Property Purchase	£1,500
Refurbishment Costs	£50,000
Furniture, white Goods & accessories	£10,000
Agent sourcing Fees	£2,500
Architect & Planning/building regs fees	£2,500
Misc. & unexpected Expenses	£2,500
Bridge Loan Interest @ 8% for 4 months	£5,600
Bridge Loan arrangement fees @ 2% of loan value	£4,200
HMO Loan arrangement fees @ 2% of loan value	£6,480
Total Costs	£386,280

Bridge Loan @ 70% of property value to purchase	£210,000
Capital required to purchase & develop property	£169,800
HMO valuation @ 35% higher value	£405,000
HMO Loan to New Valuation @ 80% LTV	£324,000
Capital remaining in investment post HMO refinancing	**£62,280**
Rental Income	
Annual Income	£37,200
Rental Monthly	£3,100
HMO Loan repayments @ 4% per annum interest	£1,080
Voids @ 5%	£155
Lettings Fee @ 8% of rental income	£236
Utilities (gas/electric/water) & council tax	£375
Accountancy Fees	£60
Internet	£50
Cleaning	£50
Building Insurance	£30
Total Costs	£2,036
Operating costs & debt payments as percentage of gross rental income	65.7%
Gross yield on total Investment	**9.7%**
Net Income per month (before tax)	**£1,064**
Return on remaining capital	**20.5%**

Note: Example 3 has a lower return on capital @ 20.5% because of the 'bridge loan' costs. However, by using a Bridge loan your initial capital outlay reduces from £370,000 to £176,280. Please also **Note** the total capital required is £169,800, this is calculated as follows: total costs are

£386,280 less Bridge Loan £210,000 less HMO arrangement fees of £6,480 as this is payable when the property is refinanced after the redevelopment.

Gross Rents Increase 300%

When a single unit dwelling is converted into an HMO in out of London locations the gross rental increases are in the region of 300%. Examples given earlier in the book are Oxford Road in Swindon had a rental valuation of £1,000 per month as a single unit let. This would be plus bills paid by the tenant, as a converted HMO the rental achieved was £3,250 including bills. Another example is Cavendish Avenue, Eastbourne the rental valuation was again circa £1,000 per month, the rent achieved as an HMO is £2,900 per month including bills.

The reason for this is that the same single dwelling accommodates multiple tenancies after conversion into an HMO, hence a potential tripling of gross rent.

Using Leverage to Build a Property Portfolio

Earlier in the chapter I gave you an insight into how to use a bank loan to take back a significant portion of your initial capital investment. On a larger scale one can build a property portfolio from refinancing each property that you buy and convert into an HMO. I must warn you that this is a greater risk strategy as your indebtedness increases, so that if interest rates go up too high you may not be able to afford your loan repayments, and the same is the case if you have low occupancy rates your income may not cover the bank repayments. Below is an example of how leveraging can assist your property portfolio expansion. I am using the same financial example as previously demonstrated.

Property 1 Cash no Debt

Using the example from the previous pages, the total investment is £370,000. Therefore, you have invested £370,000 of your own capital.

Next Step- Refinance post development with an HMO loan at an HMO property revaluation of £405,000. Loan is 80% LTV; therefore, this will allow cash out from the property of £324,000. Capital remaining in the investment £46,000. With this you now have an operational, cash generating property, plus £324,000 in capital to do the same again with the purchase of your property 2, and again with property 3. However please note each time the amount of capital refinanced will be less. This is the leveraging and refinancing property portfolio model.

Note – For the sake of simplicity in explanation I have not deducted the arrangement fees from the loan on your capital at each refinancing.

Follow Your Money

You have to **follow your money** – not checking on the properties is a lose situation, checking is a win win. Visit your property on a regular basis, I normally do a visit every 6 weeks, speak with the agents to get an update on occupation rates, general trends. When you see your tenants seek their thoughts and see how they are doing, whether they are generally happy with their tenancy. Ask if there is anything missing, the maintenance status. It shows you care and respect your tenant.

"Treat Tenants as Clients"
Sadly, this is often forgotten! If you go to a restaurant and you get bad service, you will not go back? The same applies to staying in a hotel, service from an accountant, store, boutique, pretty much anywhere else! Then why are tenants not treated like customers to be respected, listened to, and cared about? Too often landlords are quick to react when a rent payment date is missed, however look the other way when damp permeates the property or when an old boiler needs to be fixed, and they even evict tenants when they ask for improvements to shabby accommodation. Whenever you spend money on your rental property, you are spending on an asset you own from which you are lucky enough to derive a passive income, and importantly it's also someone's home!

"Respect Your Tenants"

This may sound corny, to respect your tenant, but it's true. I have tenants who pay £8,000 per month for a luxury house to others paying £400 per month for a room in an HMO. What they all have in common is that they are respected, their accommodation is well maintained and in good decorative order. If anything within the property goes wrong, it is fixed immediately. There is no discrimination between a higher rent paying tenant and a lower one. They are equal as people and tenants, whether a large house tenant, a flat renter or a small room HMO occupant, in each case it is their home, a place to be safe and secure....

"Treating Tenants Like Clients Pays Dividends"

Don't treat your tenants like fools. I have been a landlord, both residential and commercial, for the past 25 years. Most tenants respect a landlord who looks after them and the property they live in. On several occasions I have made friendships from my landlord/tenant relationships.

From my many experiences with tenants I have very rarely had issues with disruptive or non-performing tenants. They see me as a responsible landlord, one that is responsive and communicative. Therefore, if a tenant has paid late, I want to know why and show understanding and work with them. They may have lost their job. However, this does not mean I am a charitable organisation. Rents have to be paid and on time, so I am always checking the account on payment dates.

When a tenant has a nicely decorated, well maintained property, with a responsive and responsible landlord they also react and communicate in such a way. The tenants stay longer, therefore there are less void periods, and are willing to pay higher rents. They are also committed to taking care of the property.

HMO House Rules

If you are managing your own HMOs it's very important to have House Rules. This can be in addition to the Tenancy Agreement that the tenants sign.

When you have multiple occupants of a property, they are sharing the same communal space and the facilities. Therefore, they must be aware and show respect to the other tenant's quiet enjoyment of their space.

Below are some ideas for the House Rules / Dos & Don'ts for tenants.

You must <u>not do</u> the following.

1. Alter or add anything to the outside or structure of the property, or the furniture, fixtures and household belongings that are on the list that you and we signed. You must not bring into the property any furniture, fixtures or household belongings, which do not meet the Furniture and Furnishings (Fire) (Safety) Regulations. You can get information about these regulations from your local Trading Standards Office.

2. Anything which may be a nuisance or annoy neighbours. You must not play any radio, CD, record player, television or musical instrument in a way that will cause a nuisance, annoy the neighbours or be heard outside your home between 11pm and 7.30am.

3. Bring bicycles, motorcycles, and prams into the property without our permission, in writing (which we will not unreasonably withhold).

4. Bring any furniture into the house without our permission, in writing (which we will not unreasonably withhold).

5. Tamper with any fire precautions.

6. Hang pictures or posters on the walls without our permission, in writing (which we will not unreasonably withhold).

7. Use Blu-tack or any similar type of adhesive on the walls.

8. Sublet the property or any part of it or give up the property or any part of it to someone else.

9. Transfer the tenancy to someone else without our permission, in writing (which we will not unreasonably withhold).

10. Carry on any profession, trade or business in the property.

11. Display any permanent notice on the property.

12. Use the property as anything other than a home.

13. Block, or allow guests to obstruct, any of the shared areas.

14. Dry washing inside the property, except in a ventilated room suitable for such purposes.

15. Use any paraffin, Kerosene, portable gas heater and electric heaters.

16. Tell us about any repairs or faults that we are responsible for in the Room or at the Property as soon as you notice them.

Things that you <u>must do</u> below.

1. Take reasonable precautions to keep all drains, sanitary apparatus, water and waste pipes, air vents, flues and ducts free of obstruction.

2. Clear, or pay for the clearance of, any blockage or overflow when any occur in any of the drains, sinks, toilets or waste pipes if the blockage is caused by the negligence or misuse by you or your guests.

3. Pay the cost of repairing any damage to appliances, fixtures and fittings that occurs from misuse, neglect or carelessness by you or your guests.

4. Pay for damage to doors and windows if the police break into the Property as a result of any criminal or suspected criminal activity by you or your guests.

5. Pay our reasonable costs for any items belonging to us that you accidentally or purposely damage. If damage or breakages are reported and no one comes forward to pay then the cost will be

split equally between all the tenants at the Property, the proper proportion of which you will pay us.

It is important that you state as a <u>landlord what you must do too,</u> below is a suggested list.

We agree to do the following.

1. Keep the property insured against fire and other usual comprehensive risks as long as insurance cover is available.
2. Let you have free access to the steps, entrance hall, stairs and all shared areas and keep those areas clean, light and in good condition.
3. Be responsible for servicing and maintaining any gas heating system and making sure that all gas appliances within the property are checked by a Corgi-registered technician every year, in line with the Gas Safety (Installation and Use) Regulations 1994.
4. Be responsible for making sure that any furniture we provide keeps to the Furniture and Furnishings (Fire) (Safety) Regulations.
5. Give you back any part of the rent that you have paid for any period that the property could not be lived in because of fire or any other danger that we are insured for.
6. Keep the structure and outside of the property in good repair.
7. Keep the gas, water, electricity, space-heating and water-heating installations in good repair and proper working order.
8. Refund any rent you have paid which relates to a rental period which starts after the tenancy ends. We are allowed to take from this refund any rent or other money you owe us.
9. If we need to serve any notice on you, we will deliver it by hand or send it to you by first-class post to the property address. This means that notices are served on you once they are put through your letterbox, even if you do not receive them because you have

moved. If you give us another address to send notices to, any notice will be validly served at that address, if it is posted by first-class post or left at that address.

10. If you need to serve any notice on us, they must be delivered by hand or sent by post to the following address.

Troublesome Tenants

Most tenants are responsible and respectful of the property they live in and follow all the rules. However, there is always going to be a bad apple, and with difficult and troublesome tenants it's even more important to keep the line of communication open. I make sure I meet them face-to-face, so they see I am accessible and that I care about my property and any genuine grievance they may have. However, if after several meetings and, most important, written reminders, the tenant is unresponsive to my reasonable requests and they are not performing on their side of the deal, not paying rent or continuously disturbing the other tenants, I have to put my foot down and take action. I have evicted tenants and on occasion sent in the bailiffs to repossess the property. You should follow the below procedure to be within the law:

Section 21 notice of seeking possession

You can use a Section 21 notice to evict your tenants either:

- after a fixed term tenancy ends - if there's a written contract
- during a tenancy with no fixed end date - known as a 'periodic' tenancy

Giving tenants a Section 21 notice

You must give your tenants the Section 21 notice by filling in form 6a if the tenancy started or was renewed after 30 September 2015.

Otherwise, you can write your own Section 21 notice. If it's a periodic tenancy, you must explain that you're giving notice under Section 21 of the Housing Act 1988.

How much notice you need to give?

A Section 21 notice must always give your tenants at least 2 months' notice to leave your property. If it's a periodic tenancy, you must also let your tenants stay for any additional time covered by their final rent payment.

After you give notice

Keep proof that you gave notice to your tenants - either:

- fill in the certification of service form (N215)
- write "served by [your name] on [the date]" on the notice

Section 8 notice of seeking possession

To give your tenants notice using a Section 8, you must fill in a 'Notice seeking possession of a property let on an assured tenancy or an assured agricultural occupancy'. Specify on the notice which terms of the tenancy they've broken.

You can give between 2 weeks' and 2 months' notice depending on which terms they've broken.

You can apply to the court for a possession order if your tenants do not leave by the specified date.

Today's accomplishments
were yesterday's impossibilities

- Robert H. Schuller

Picking the Right Managing Agents

As explained earlier I go out of my way to find good agents, this is particularly important if the property is located in a town I do not live in. The agent in some ways becomes my unofficial partner, so it's important to form a good relationship with the right agent, they source my properties and assist with local contractors and most importantly manage the properties. I make sure the agent has the right attitude not just to the client, which is me but also to the real client which is the tenant. Are they responsive and caring towards the tenants needs and requests, but also firm on making sure all tenants adhere to the House Rules and collecting the rents on time and crediting my account quickly and accurately. Prior to making a decision on who should manage my property I check the properties they are managing, speak with some of their tenants and get references from existing landlords.

I normally agree an 8-10% agency fee for a full management service and try to use independent local firms with good solid experience of managing HMOs.

SOURCING FEES & AGENTS

I do use the services of sourcing agents as they provide a very important task, which is finding me property purchase opportunities. I have located properties without sourcing agents however you can only search areas you are located in or know well, and hence limit your opportunities. As I invest in many differing areas, I need local knowledge and that means using credible sourcing agents, I often have several agents looking for properties in different areas.

A sourcing agent is usually a freelance estate agent/ property consultant or a local estate agency, they charge between 1% - 3% dependent on the deal size. I would strongly recommend using their very valuable services.

Care Home to HMO Conversion

My latest HMO project involved a development project in Wiltshire. This was an ex-residential care home, a detached large property circa 3,600 square feet of internal space. When the property was purchased nearly all the rooms had en-suite shower WCs which helped to reduce the conversion costs. The project needed planning permission to change the use from a C2 class to HMO. The planning application was carried out by my architect and it took 2 months to conclude on the planning. There was some risk as the purchase was not subject to planning, but before the exchange a thorough due diligence was carried out. The conclusion was that planning permission could be given.

The property has been completely refurbished, and in part re-configured to create new 2nd kitchen and shower/wc. We carried out complete electrical re-wiring, fire security improvements, plumbing, flooring, en-suites upgraded, creation of further shower-rooms, new kitchen units and the conversion of a wing of the house into a self-contained HMO studio unit with own entrance. In total we have 11 rooms, 10 are en-suite shower / WC and one off-suite. The local council has specified the number of parking spaces, where the refuse bins will be located and the type of bike parking stands that are needed. As this is a large HMO, the conversion and build took circa 14 weeks. The property is located 10 minutes' walk to the town centre and main line rail station, 2 minutes to a local hospital.

The tenant base is the hospital, local employment centres such as Dyson in Tetbury Hill, Malmesburyor, and commercial employment hubs like Bristol and Swindon. The business angle for this purchase was the fact that this was too a small sized property for a care home, which meant it had become not viable with rising operational costs, therefore when it came to buyers new care home operators were not interested. It also was too large and complicated for a conversion back into a single unit large house, so residential buyers were put off buying it. Hence, we were able to purchase it with a sizeable discount. In respect of the amount paid on a pound per square foot basis this house was 35-40% below market price.

The refurbishment costs were lower per square foot, because there was no structural works or extensions and the en-suites were already in situ. Our research into the town had shown that there is demand for HMO rooms and a lack of supply, with only a handful of HMO operators. Within 6 weeks of completion of the development we had 100% occupancy.

Below existing floor plans when property was purchased

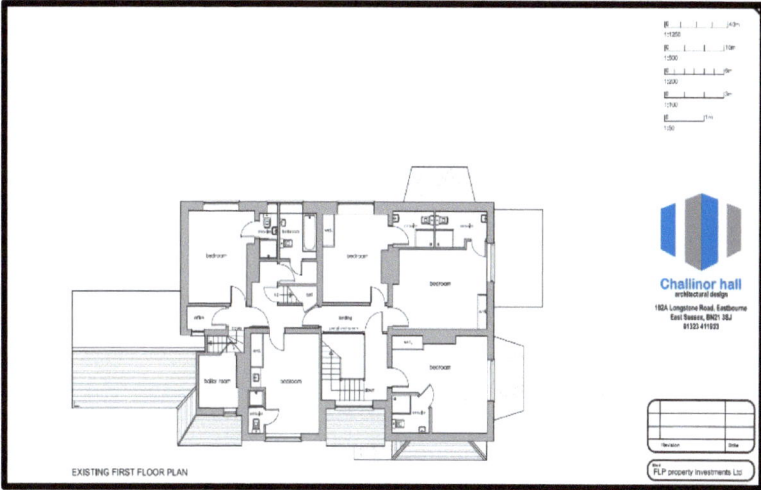

EXISTING FIRST FLOOR PLAN

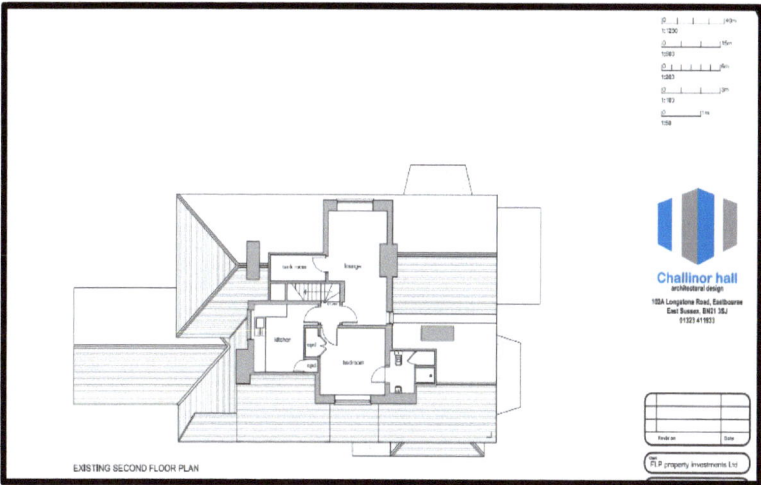

EXISTING SECOND FLOOR PLAN

Below floorplans are when the development was completed.

PROPOSED GROUND FLOOR PLAN

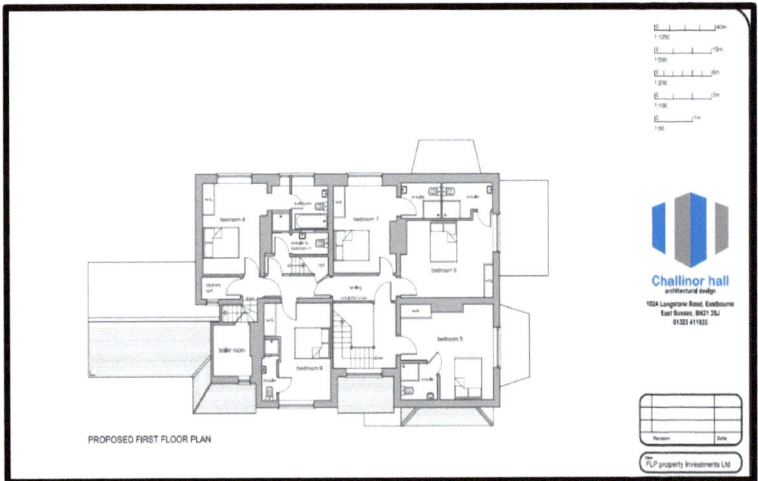

PROPOSED FIRST FLOOR PLAN

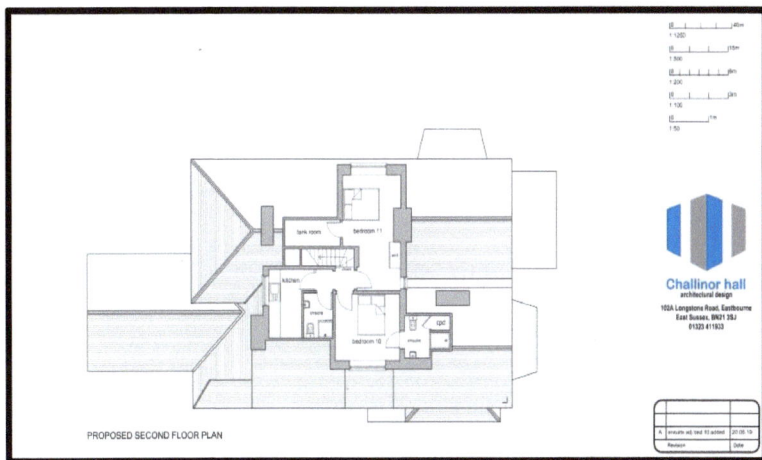

PROPOSED SECOND FLOOR PLAN

Photographs of completed Chippenham project care-home to HMO conversion

155

You don't have to be
great to start, but you
have to start to be great

- Zig Ziglar

Downsizing UK

Over the past two decades property prices have risen in real terms (factoring inflation) by 152%, however wages for 25 to 34-year-olds have only risen by 22% over the same period. Therefore, fewer people buy, more rent and rents have gone up, in fact they have doubled in the past 10 years.

This has meant a boom for building smaller units, and conversion of large properties to multiple flats, some as mentioned before are office to residential conversions. With this downsizing boom has been the growth in the HMO market, what was a casual house sharing concept 20 years ago is now recognized as an investment model which is licensed and regulated and has in place specific bank funding.

Estimates have put the number of new homes needed in England at between 240,000 and 340,000 per year, accounting for new household formation and a backlog of existing need for suitable housing. In 2017/18, the total housing stock in England increased by around 222,000 homes

Unless new property build is increased to match the demand, house prices will not go down and most likely increase as will the rents. This will mean an increase in demand for HMO rentals.

CHANGING TRENDS, RENTING NOT OWNING

The UK has for a long time been a property-owning country, however in the past 20 years, average house prices have grown by about seven times faster than the average incomes of young adults, according to the Institute for Fiscal Studies.

Those born in the late 1980s are much less likely to be homeowners in their late 20s than their immediate predecessors. About a 25% of those born towards the end of Margaret Thatcher's government owned their own home at the age of 27 compared with a third born at the start of the decade and 43% of those born in the late 1970s.

About 1.75 million people who rent their homes do not believe they will ever be able to buy, an increase of 50% since 2010.

A fifth of the UK population now lives in privately rented accommodation, the English Housing Survey has revealed in its latest report for 2016/2017, accounting for 4.7 million households. This figure has doubled from the 10% of people living in the PRS back in 1996/1997 and is a huge leap over the past decade from 12% in 2006/2007.

With this changing trend to rent rather than buy, many are pinning the blame on the flailing housing market and out of reach house prices forcing people to remain in rented accommodation as they are unable to buy a home.

Sub-Standard Housing

There is so much sub-standard housing in the UK, this is not just to do with the lack of supply but also with a lack of regulation.

Slum landlords have to be penalised and face the consequences of their lack of action in maintaining good habitable standards in their properties. Tenants expectations have to be raised, and the laws changed where tenants cannot be just turfed out because they have complained about essential maintenance in a property.

I have been a landlord for well over 20 years, but I sincerely support the tenant's rights, decent affordable housing should be available to all in a country such as the UK, the 5th biggest economy in the world.

NEWS ARTICLES

- **BBC News Report 22 Jan 2016**

The scourge of substandard housing in the UK. More people in the UK are living in private rented accommodation than ever before. However, one in every six homes is considered hazardous. Now, an extra £5m in government funding is being announced to tackle this problem in England.

The Guardian Article 13th April 2019

Exclusive analysis of official figures by the academic duo at the forefront of research into the private rental sector, Julie Rugg and David Rhodes, shows that 90% of the 1.4 million households renting on low incomes in England are being put at risk by harmful living conditions and/or pushed further into poverty and possible eviction by rents they cannot afford.

Nearly 30% are living in non-decent homes, 10% are living in overcrowded properties and 85% are in "after housing cost poverty", which means their rent pushes them below the poverty line.

"Worryingly the evidence tells us there is a growing residual slum tenure for private rented-sector households on low incomes, whose needs are being neglected by policymakers," says Rugg, from York University. "Poorer renters are much more likely to be living with damp, disrepair and sometimes life-threatening hazards – as well as rents they can only pay by cutting back on essentials like food or heating."

Below examples of Slum Housing in the UK

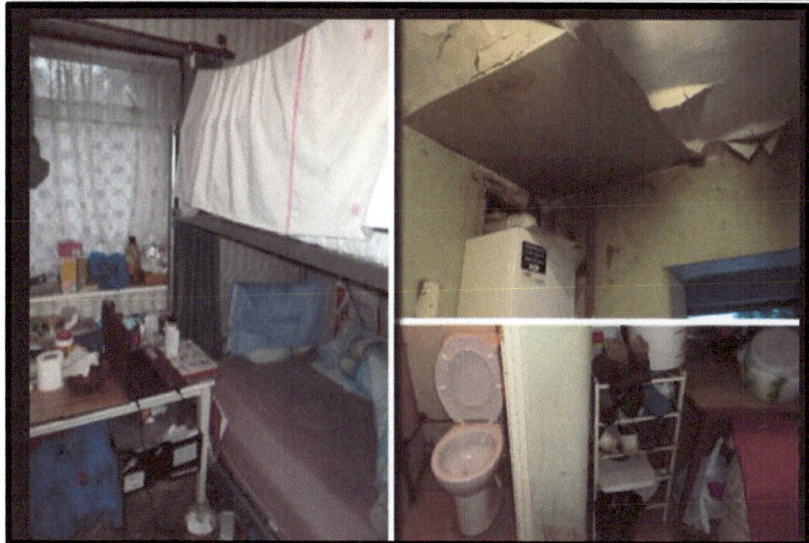

Integrity is the most
valuable and respected
quality of leadership.
Always keep your word

Buying Properties in Companies

I buy all my properties in companies, and ideally each company owns one property. There are many advantages to this.

Why buy a property in a company?

- Your liability is limited to the company assets not your other assets. In the unfortunate and unforeseen situation that you are facing financial challenges, your creditors are limited in their actions to "Only" the asset that the company owns, unless you have given personal guarantees (PGs).
- You can offset your interest payment against your income. It is an expense, whereas if the property is owned by a person this is not allowed. The law recently changed, by 2020 you won't be able to deduct any of your mortgage interest payment from your rental income before paying tax – instead, the entire sum of your interest payment will then qualify for a 20% tax relief. This means that a landlord getting £10,000 in rent and paying £9,000 in mortgage interest payments will end up paying tax on the full £10,000 – though the amount will still depend on your tax bracket. You will then be able to deduct £1,800 from your tax bill due to the 20% tax credit, leaving you with the final overall tax bill on your rental income.
- You can sell the property via selling its shares. Therefore, the buyer's stamp duty will be far less, currently 0.5% rather than below rates. This is with the proviso that if you have a loan your lender must be notified of the change in the shareholding within the company.
- Multiple people can buy shares in your property proportionate to their investment.

STAMP DUTY RATES

Property or lease premium or transfer value	SDLT rate
Up to £125,000	Zero
The next £125,000 (the portion from £125,001 to £250,000)	2%
The next £675,000 (the portion from £250,001 to £925,000)	5%
The next £575,000 (the portion from £925,001 to £1.5 million)	10%
The remaining amount (the portion above £1.5 million)	12%

- Plus, you will pay an extra 3% if you are buying not as your main home, as a second or more properties.

TAX & WEALTH MANAGEMENT

This is a very important area of investment, and property tax is very specialised. It is essential to get a tax advisor that specialises on property investments.

How you are taxed on your property investments will depend on how they are legally owned, how you take out your money from them and what other sources of income you have.

Be prudent and get specialist tailored advice…

YOUR LAWYER

Picking the right law firm and lawyer is a very important decision. If you do not have a lawyer choose one through recommendation. In my 3 decades of business experience I have used dozens of different law firms both in the UK and internationally.

The three most important characteristics I have found in a good lawyer are:

1. Do they know their specialist law well?

2. Their response time, on important matters I like my lawyer to respond within 2 hours unless they are away.

3. A lawyer must be flexible and street smart, meaning there is a lot of stop start and holding positions in purchasing property. As I earlier mentioned when I have agreed a purchase, I always notify my lawyer immediately. In some instances, to secure the purchase prior to financing I use the lawyer in a holding position where my lawyer has the sales contract, as only one interested purchasing party can have the sales contract, therefore one can delay a purchase by a few weeks whilst you are organising funding or carrying out further due diligence.

One of the lessons that I
grew up with was to always
stay true to yourself and never
let what somebody else says
distract you from your goal

- Michelle Obama

Capital Growth Versus High Yield

Capital Growth

I am always asked this question; investors want to know how they can have good capital growth and high yields too. This is difficult but not impossible.

Capital growth is usually in areas, cities and towns where there is high inward migration and capital inflows where demand outstrips supply for an extended period, for at least 5 years plus. This means property prices go up.

Another factor is low interest rates and high loan to value ratios, which make it easier for 1st time buyers to get on the property ladder.

A third important factor is government and local authority regeneration schemes, here large sums are invested by the government in partnership with private equity to develop and regenerate areas within a city. This creates a buzz through local and national media and PR companies which are feeders to property forums and property agencies both national and international.

Examples of Capital Growth Cities

Manchester

House prices in Manchester have increased more than anywhere else in the UK, exceeding the UK average in five out of the last six years.

This culminated in a significant gap in 2017, when the average house value in Manchester rose 11%, against a regional average of 6%, and a UK average of just 5%.

Manchester also leads the way in house price inflation when compared with all other core UK cities. In the 12 months to July 2018 prices in Manchester rose just under 9%, compared to Leeds at just 3.8%. In London house price inflation saw a drop of 1%. Greater

Manchester is the UK's largest and fastest growing economy outside of London.

Seen as the regional centre for finance, commercial and retail with world class transport links, Manchester is now one of the best cities in Europe to do business in. Major corporations such as the Co-operative Group, Amazon, the Royal Bank of Scotland, the BBC and ITV have all chosen to establish key operations within the city. The relocation and start-ups of these major corporations and small independent businesses has resulted in the creation of new jobs.

It is expected that around 3,100 new jobs will be created per year across Manchester to 2034. Many of these jobs will be high salaries based in the city centre. As a result, Manchester's population is anticipated to grow by 3,500 people per year over the same period creating an ever-growing demand for housing.

A fundamental driver in the popularity of the North West as a region in which to invest has been price. Price points perceived as affordable, particularly from an emergent overseas market and a somewhat overpriced, oversaturated London investor market, have proved popular with buy-to-let investors acquiring new-build and second hand stock. Manchester grew its population by 19% between 2000 – 2011.

Despite the significant regeneration of Manchester that has already taken place, it does not look like things are coming to a halt any time soon. In the next five years there are plans to overhaul three stations in Manchester, including Oxford Road, Piccadilly and Victoria. Not only are the stations going to be redeveloped, but also the surrounding areas.

Reading

Reading flats outperform the property market on average by 29% according to the Land Registry's latest House Price Index for Reading and the surrounding locality, the value of apartments/flats are rising at a faster rate than terraced/town houses, semi-detached properties and even detached property.

The average property price in 1995 in Reading was £72,872, today in 2019 the average property price is £346,619, that's 480% in 24 years which equates to an average growth of 20% per annum (without factoring for inflation).

This has occurred due to much town centre regeneration, including such as the last major plot of Reading Prison, which will be developed and the new train line going into Green Park. The fastest journey time is 24 minutes. There are 253 trains per day travelling from London Paddington to Reading.

So Reading is a major commuter town, I'm sure you would of loved to have invested in Reading, 20 plus years ago, for example if we take the fact that back in 1995 the average property cost £72,872 and you had put a 20% deposit to purchase this property, the remainder coming from bank debt. This would have meant your £14,457 (20% of property cost) would have made you **2397%**, which is 100% per annum over 24 years, what a fantastic return!

The knack is to locate an up and coming area to invest. This is where research, research and even more research is key. Luckily, we have a lot of information online, government reports, property forums, property consultancy data, and more. On top of online research, you should contact real estate agents and local property consultants, and actual visits to these areas, walk around talk to local people and shop owners and get a feel of what the town has to offer. **Finally follow the money as they say**, see what smart savvy investors are doing, which areas are large credible development companies investing in and building.

Yield

The "yield" of a property tells you how much of an annual return you are likely to get on your investment. It is calculated by expressing a year's rental income as a percentage of how much the property cost.

The higher the yield the better the return on your invested capital. Usually high yields are in low capital cost properties, therefore the cheaper the property the higher should be the yield. This does work conversely with capital growth, as lower priced properties tend to be less desirable areas and hence the growth usually is less.

In central London, Prime property yields are as low as 1.5% - 2.5%, in London outer suburbs it is 4-5%. Commuter belt towns up to an hour from London by train, the yields are 5-6 %, HMOs are up to 10% - 12% yield. In the northern towns the yields can be as high as 10%, with HMOs up to 15%.

Leaders set high standards.
Refuse to tolerate mediocrity
or poor performance

The Top 50 Buy to Let Yields (single units not HMO)

Location	Percentage of Rental Housing Stock	Average House Price	Average Rent (Monthly)	Average Rent (Annual)	Rental Yield (gross)
Southampton	23.42%	£138,311	£901	£10,812	7.82%
Blackpool	24.16%	£75,943	£494	£5,928	7.81%
Kingston upon Hull	19.02%	£69,519	£450	£5,400	7.77%
Manchester	26.85%	£102,631	£650	£7,800	7.60%
Nottingham	21.64%	£83,313	£524	£6,288	7.55%
Coventry	19.02%	£104,970	£624	£7,488	7.13%
Slough	23.07%	£171,581	£975	£11,700	6.82%
Oxford	26.11%	£244,893	£1,375	£16,500	6.74%
Liverpool	21.75%	£91,012	£498	£5,976	6.57%
Portsmouth	22.28%	£141,971	£775	£9,300	6.55%
Cardiff	20.32%	£140,882	£750	£9,000	6.39%
Cambridge	23.91%	£179,699	£949	£11,388	6.34%
Southwark	22.22%	£401,405	£2,058	£24,696	6.15%
Luton	21.27%	£127,473	£650	£7,800	6.12%
Newham	32.62%	£229,141	£1,126	£13,512	5.90%
Leicester	21.28%	£112,226	£550	£6,600	5.88%
Bournemouth	28.21%	£170,493	£825	£9,900	5.81%
Enfield	21.18%	£261,163	£1,200	£14,400	5.51%

Brighton and Hove	28.04%	£229,622	£1,049	£12,588	5.48%
Brent	28.82%	£337,723	£1,517	£18,204	5.39%
Forest Heath	21.80%	£179,699	£795	£9,540	5.31%
Torbay	21.43%	£139,168	£598	£7,176	5.16%
Southend-on-Sea	20.72%	£152,171	£650	£7,800	5.13%
Watford	18.89%	£240,239	£997	£11,964	4.98%
Bristol, City of	22.11%	£169,425	£695	£8,340	4.92%
Kingston upon Thames	21.04%	£333,122	£1,363	£16,356	4.91%
Reading	24.68%	£196,309	£795	£9,540	4.86%
Hounslow	22.23%	£285,927	£1,148	£13,776	4.82%
Wandsworth	30.02%	£428,987	£1,694	£20,328	4.74%
Lewisham	22.97%	£283,031	£1,101	£13,212	4.67%
Shepway	20.17%	£181,399	£695	£8,340	4.60%
Tower Hamlets	30.84%	£364,296	£1,387	£16,644	4.57%
Eastbourne	21.65%	£177,408	£675	£8,100	4.57%
Harrow	20.37%	£306,381	£1,148	£13,776	4.50%
Croydon	19.83%	£254,591	£949	£11,388	4.47%
Exeter	19.56%	£187,680	£693	£8,316	4.43%
Isles of Scilly	20.63%	£180,227	£654	£7,848	4.35%
Lincoln	19.36%	£119,076	£429	£5,148	4.32%
Redbridge	21.63%	£292,459	£1,049	£12,588	4.30%
Cheltenham	20.15%	£170,573	£598	£7,176	4.21%

Ipswich	18.75%	£153,163	£524	£6,288	4.11%
Richmond upon Thames	20.55%	£485,496	£1,647	£19,764	4.07%
Westminster	37.56%	£767,112	£2,578	£30,936	4.03%
Norwich	20.10%	£179,699	£598	£7,176	3.99%
Camden	30.46%	£646,043	£2,145	£25,740	3.98%
Hastings	27.19%	£177,408	£550	£6,600	3.72%
Haringey	30.33%	£372,278	£1,148	£13,776	3.70%
Thanet	21.96%	£181,399	£524	£6,288	3.47%
Hammersmith and Fulham	30.05%	£593,787	£1,690	£20,280	3.42%
Kensington and Chelsea	33.97%	£1,090,943	£3,033	£36,396	3.34%

Leaders think and talk
about the solutions.
Followers think and talk
about the problems.

Build to Rent Model

In the past ten years, the number of UK residents renting property has doubled, and roughly 20% of UK households (as high as 30% in London) are in private rented accommodation. It is estimated that a third of these tenants will continue to rent, due to the rising cost of home ownership. Research suggests that one in three millennials (adults born between the early 1980s and 2000s) will stay in private renting beyond retirement.

In 2017, the burgeoning build-to-rent market, comprising purpose-built blocks of rental homes, attracted £2.4bn in investment and is forecast to grow by a further 180% over the next six years.

The attraction for large pension and insurance funds, such as Legal & General, is clear. They have the capital to develop large blocks of flats, which are let out and managed long term by a single company rather than being sold to individual landlords. This provides institutional investors with a stable, long-term income stream. And for tenants, there's a promise of a more streamlined experience, with bespoke, high-quality management rather than an unreliable, individual private landlord.

Build-to-rent company Fizzy Living, for example, boasts of providing a five-star service and promises to complement the "hectic lifestyles of work-hard, play-hard professionals". Tenants are offered longer tenancies than for standard rental accommodation, with contracts of up to three years or more, and with amenities, such as gyms, communal lounges and cinema rooms.

Because build-to-rent has the potential to increase the supply of homes and improve conditions for renters, many in the property world, such as investment firm Venn Partners and consultancy Lichfield's, have touted it as a way to solve the UK housing crisis. It has also received considerable government support, including a £1bn build-to-rent fund.

RENT TO RENT MODEL

Rent to Rent is where an individual or company takes an interest in a property for a period of time from a landlord and guarantees to pay a fixed rent to the landlord. The landlord gives consent to the third party, 'the Renter', to rent the property to other tenants.

The Renter then rents the property to a sub-tenant at a higher rent to make a profit on the difference. However, if the property is vacant with no rental revenue the Renter still has to pay the fixed rent to the landlord.

The benefits of the arrangement to the landlord is that their rental income is guaranteed regardless of whether the tenants who live at the property pay the rent or if the property becomes empty.

As the Renter has taken a lease of the property, they become the landlord. This gives them the opportunity to find tenants for the property and they get to keep whatever rent the tenants pay. They generally allow more flexible arrangements with the tenants.

The most important benefit for the Renter is that you do not tie up any capital or take on any debt buying properties, your only risk is voids which you will have to pay from your own pocket.

Fractional Ownership Property Model

Fractional ownership is a method in which several unrelated parties can share in, and mitigate the risk of, ownership of a high-value tangible asset, usually a jet, yacht or piece of resort real estate. It can be done for strictly monetary reasons, but typically there is some amount of personal access involved.

Fractional Ownership vs Timeshare.

The main difference between fractional ownership and a timeshare is in the way actual equity is distributed. In a fractional ownership arrangement, the purchaser actual owns a piece of equity in the property. ... With a timeshare, ownership is not distributed.

The bad news is that not all lenders are familiar with the concept of fractional property, so you might not be able to obtain a mortgage from your neighbourhood bank. ... In fact, for the banks that do lend for these types of loans it's essentially no different from getting a mortgage on any other second home.

An example is The Hideaways Club the fractional ownership company that is celebrating 10 years of buying luxurious holiday homes all over the world for its 500 or so members to share in owning and using.

The Hideaways Club has spent £60m on buying 54 properties worldwide, with little leverage. The average purchase price per property is around £1.2m, but it varies massively among destinations. Half that amount in Turkey or Morocco buys a palace, but you'd need to double the budget for something of a similar quality in the south of France.

It is also a cheaper way to holiday in this type of property. Members pay an Annual Cost Contribution (ACC), which ranges from £3,750 to £15,000 depending on their share type, and that covers the cost of running and improving the properties.

SMART HOME TECHNOLOGY

Smart thermostats are a new bit of kit that connects your heating system to the internet – letting you change the temperature or switch your heating off from your smartphone or other device when you're out and about, or with your computer. You need an internet connection to use them of course.

Remember that these are different from smart meters - which most energy firms are currently offering to install for free. Plus, unlike smart meters, you install or arrange installation of smart thermostats yourself – so it doesn't matter which energy provider supplies your energy.

The main advantage to the landlord is you are in control of heating, stopping the over usage of radiators being on all the time, you could be thousands of miles away but can adjust your rented property thermostats. This can potentially save hundreds or even thousands of pounds a year.

SOLAR PANELS

More than 800,000 British households use solar panels to reduce their energy bills. Solar panel electricity systems, also known as photovoltaics (PV), capture the sun's energy using photovoltaic cells.

These cells don't need direct sunlight to work – they can still generate some electricity on a cloudy day. The cells convert the sunlight into electricity, which can be used to run household appliances and lighting. The benefits of solar electricity are:

Cut your electricity bills. Sunlight is free, so once you've paid for the initial installation, your electricity costs will be reduced.

Cut your carbon footprint. Solar electricity is green renewable energy and doesn't release any harmful carbon dioxide or other pollutants. A typical home solar PV system could save around 1.3 to 1.6 tonnes of carbon per year (depending where you are within the UK).

The National Energy Trust has estimated that a typical family house will save on average £240 per annum, however this figure has to be multiplied several times dependent on the size of your HMO, with multiple electric showers and half a dozen or more tenants. Therefore, with a larger 12 room HMO we are looking at potentially thousands of pounds saving a year.

A 4kWp system can generate around 4,200 kilowatt hours of electricity a year in the south of England – that's the same amount of electricity as it takes to turn the London Eye 56 times. It will save around 1.6 tonnes of carbon dioxide every year. A 4kWp system in Scotland can generate about 3,400 kilowatt hours of electricity a year – that's the same amount of electricity as it takes to turn the Falkirk Wheel 2,200 times. It will save approximately 1.3 tonnes of carbon dioxide every year.

The average domestic solar PV system is 4kWp and costs around £6,200 (including VAT at 5 per cent).

Environmentally Sustainable Development
Sustainable development can be classified as development that meets the needs of the present without compromising the ability of future generations. ... As the concept developed, it has shifted to focus more on economic development, social development and environmental protection for future generations. Sustainable economic growth while promoting jobs and stronger economies.

All of the above and more while tackling the effects of climate change, pollution and other environmental factors that can harm and do harm people's health, livelihoods and lives. Sustainability to include health of the land, air and sea.

The three pillars of sustainability.
So, to achieve true sustainability we need to balance economic, social and environmental sustainability factors in equal harmony. These may be defined as: Environmental Sustainability: Environmental sustainability means that we are living within the means of our natural resources.

There are developers who are participating in this space. Leeds-based firm Citu, for example, is making a splash with its low-carbon, community-focused sites. Their stated purpose is to tackle climate change. The biggest challenge of our generation. Carbon emissions are generated by buildings, transport and energy use, and they want to tackle all three by being innovative.

As well as its base in Beeston, Leeds, Citu has a site in Little Kelham, Sheffield. It is currently selling homes in the Climate Innovation District – in Hunslet, south Leeds – the UK's biggest urban sustainable development. The 700 one to four-bedroom, low-carbon homes start from £150,000.

Last year, Citu began production of carbon-negative, timber-framed residential units, built at its factory and designed to be 10 times more efficient than the average modern UK home. The properties will have lower heat transmittance than standard brick-built homes, will use less energy and cost less to run. What little heating is needed will come via a heat recovery system, which transfers warmth from outgoing air to incoming fresh air. The homes will also have green roofs, rainwater collection and photovoltaic panels, which will be connected to a smart grid monitoring the community's electricity use.

On a smaller scale, but no less ambitious, is LivEco, which is building sustainable properties at Great House Farm, Cardiff. This site is an eight-acre former farm with 36 homes, a mix of apartments and houses, the last 13 of which are about to go on sale priced from £354,000. The properties have a rustic-chic appearance, as well as having a low carbon footprint. All benefit from super-insulated thermal wood cladding, high-performance windows and doors, heat recovery systems, and green roofs, planted with sedum. Buyers are primarily interested in the savings they can make by reducing energy use, rather than the features.

The future is in 'Environmentally Sustainable Development', now development companies choose to enter this niche sector of home building, in the future it may become mandatory by governments!

INVESTING WITH PARTNERS

I'm a great believer in working as a team, whether with agents, tenants, brokers, builders, maintenance contractors, and this is the same with silent partner investors. I have invested in property with partners, they rely on my property knowledge and expertise, contacts and ability to conclude on residential projects.

The key with partners is to discuss everything from the start, be 100% transparent, sign a clear mutually beneficial and protective partnership agreement that says exactly what you have agreed and update them on a regular basis as the project progresses.

Why Have Partners?

Firstly you are doing them a favour as ordinarily they would not enter into these lucrative property deals/projects, however it is important from the start to clearly inform them that there are no guarantees and that there could be losses and they need to check independently all the information you have given them.

From your perspective you will be either putting less of your own capital or none at all, as clearly your knowledge and credibility will make the project happen. Plus, your experience and credit worthiness is an important factor in facilitating the debt from the banks, who often want experienced operators.

With the above investment model I charge a fee plus share of profits, this is the same principle both for HMO investing and property developing.

PROPERTY CONSULTANCY

An alternative to investing or partnering can be working as a consultant. This means giving expertise and knowledge without being part of the investment structure, I don't invest any money nor take on any liabilities such as debt repayments or personal guarantees. The investor funds the project with own capital and bank funding and take on all responsibilities to third parties such as builders.

I advise and oversee the whole project and charge a consultancy fee.

Practice golden rule management in everything you do. Manage others the way you would like to be managed

THE JOY OF PROPERTY INVESTING

Our home, be it a mansion, house, flat or a room is a very important part of our lives. To own a property is a privilege and should be valued and appreciated.

It is estimated that 150 million people are homeless worldwide. Habitat for Humanity estimated in 2015 that 1.6 billion people around the world live in "inadequate shelter". Twenty per cent of the world's population lack adequate housing.

As a landlord, I and many others like me provide a very important service to our tenants the clients, we provide them with a home, it should be somewhere safe, clean and well maintained. Remember that next time you speak with one of your tenants they are not just a number but a person who is paying you a rent that gives you a passive income, you could be relaxing on a beach in the Caribbean sunning yourself and your income is being credited into your account without you lifting a finger…

The UK is a country with transparency and has a solid legal framework to support a sophisticated property sector, with many models available for investing in property. This is the same for bank funding for property purchases, developments and long-term rental investments.

I have enjoyed the past 25 plus years investing in property, the many people that I have met and connected with, the opportunities that were created for me and my partners. The income generated from these investments have paid my bills, allowed me and my family the freedoms to do what we want when we want.

I do hope this book goes someway in explaining the complexities and mysteries that property investing may have for a newcomer going into this business especially with their hard-earned savings. My aim is to lessen your risk and increase your chances of making a better return on your capital through a thorough understanding of the subject matter.

In summary the most important key points to consider in investing and managing your properties are as below:

Golden Rules to Investing & Managing Your Properties

- Research, research and more research, do your homework about the area you are investing, the actual property, the build costs. Research does not cost you anything except your time but can save you a lot of money or make you a lot of money if you make the wrong or right decision.
- Make good connections with credible related parties, sourcing / managing agents, builders, finance brokers, architects, these people will all assist you in finding, building and managing your prized HMO asset. Without them your risks increase as will your stress levels.
- Follow your money, when developing the property, and set up a weekly reporting system so that you are being updated by your builder regularly. Visit the site often, weekly, bi-weekly or monthly, dependent on the size and complexity of the build and how well you know the build team. It's important that the builder sees you checking and caring about your property investment and for you to see the progress.
- Have good relations with your tenants, treat them with respect and as clients, respond quickly and efficiently to any of their genuine property related maintenance requests.
- Follow your monthly rental incomes and be quick off the mark if rent has not come in on time, ask why, and when it will be paid. Work with your tenants if they are having genuine difficulties such as moving jobs or unforeseen situations, they still have to pay their rent, but it can be delayed. If the tenant genuinely has lost their job and has no income, and they want to move out, allow them to break their rental agreement, try and

get all or most of the money owed to you. In my 25 plus years of being a landlord, I have never had a rent default, this is because I have worked with my tenants, even on occasion lowering their rent, be flexible and understanding, you are assisting them and yourself too.

- Visit your property regularly, I ordinarily visit every 6- 8 weeks, to see the state of repair and chat with my tenants and see if everything is fine. The tenants also see that you are caring for your property and following your money too, the property.

Closure of The Chelsea Bun

As I come to conclude this book, sadly I have had to close the Chelsea Bun café after 35 years of trading. We shut the doors for the last time on Sunday 19th May 2019!

Many customers were devastated, and some were in tears. It meant so much to a lot of people including me…a place that was a constant in an ever-changing world.

I have an independent journalist helping me get the closure news into the national papers. The story is the death of the high street and small independents.

Sometimes a restaurant is just that, a place to eat. But they can be so much more. A meeting point for friends, a gathering place for extended families, a place to do business, to get to know your neighbours, or simply a refuge in which to catch a few moments to yourself away from the rushing torrent of modern life.

Eventually restaurants like these become an integral part of the fabric of their community. For 35 years the Chelsea Bun, on Lamont Road, in the heart of West London, was exactly that.

The Chelsea Bun was a simple restaurant, unfussy and with good, freshly cooked food. Ultimately what everyone wants is something genuine: genuine food, genuine conversation, a genuine experience. The Chelsea Bun provided just that for three and a half decades.

In its heyday the place would be completely full, with a queue stretching from the shop up to the Kings Road, on many occasions 40 people deep. I valued each and every one of my patrons, whether it was a customer buying a cup of tea or a three course meal. The amount of spend was irrelevant, it was our good fortune to serve them.

For me it was a second home. I loved the place and have wonderful memories of the wonderful people I met and the many friends I made.

We closed because the lease had expired. Renewing would have meant a substantial increase in rent, which I could not afford given we were barely surviving the past years on the current rent and high business rates. This was combined with a substantial drop in business due to a proliferation of competition in the area, many of which are large corporate chains backed by invisible private equity and corporate funds, they are killing off small independent operators like myself.

I thank all the wonderful customers for making the Chelsea Bun a humble simple but 'world famous café'!

Thank you also to my wonderful staff. It could not have happened without you.

HMO REPORT – Exeter

Below is an example of an internal report which is prepared before I start the process of looking for a property in a town/city which I am not familiar with and outside my business comfort zone. I have over a dozen such reports prepared on UK towns.

LOCATION

Exeter is a cathedral city and region's capital in the Devon county in South West England.

The town comprises 13 electoral wards. The majority of the city is the Exeter constituency but two wards (St Loyes and Topsham) are in East Devon.

- Alphington
- Duryard & St James
- Exwick
- Heavitree
- Mincinglake & Whipton
- Newtown & St Leonards
- Pennsylvania
- Pinhoe
- Priory
- St David's
- St Loyes
- St Thomas
- Topsham

The local authority district of Exeter is located in south east Devon. Ten miles inland from the south coast at the head of the Exe estuary, the city is located between Teignbridge to the west and East Devon to the east and is the home of Devon County Council.

The city of Exeter was established on the eastern bank of the River Exe on a ridge of land backed by a steep hill. It is at this point that the Exe, having just been joined by to River Creedy opens onto a wide flood plain and estuary, which results in quite common flooding. Historically this was the lowest bridging point of the River Exe, which was tidal and navigable up to the city until the construction of weirs later in its history. This combined with the easily defensible higher ground of the ridge made the current location of the city a natural choice for settlement and trade. In George Oliver's *The History of the City of Exeter*, it is noted that the most likely reasons for the original settling of what would become modern Exeter was the "fertility of the surrounding countryside" and the area's "beautiful and commanding elevation [and] its rapid and navigable river". Its woodland would also have been ideal for natural resources and hunting.

POPULATION

There is an estimated 129,800 people living in Exeter and over 93% of the population is white. The largest ethnic group in the city is Chinese, with 1.7% of the population identifying as this ethnicity per the 2011 UK Census. Surprisingly, the period between the 2001 and 2011 censuses show that White British and White Irish populations were declining, while the Chinese population grew by an astounding 429%. Other Asian ethnic groups also saw an increase in their population by over 400%.

38,900 (68%) of the population is of working age (i.e. between ages of 16-64) which is above the national average of 66%. Exeter's large student population contributes to this figure.

Exeter has an employment rate of 72%, which is slightly higher than the national average of 71.4%.

The rate of unemployment in Exeter is lower at 4.9% compared to the UK rate of 5.1% and much lower when compared to England's rate of 7.9%.

Exeter is at the heart of a travel to work area of over 470,000 residents.

The population of Exeter grew by almost 7,000 (6.4%) between 2001 and 2011 which is smaller than the United Kingdom growth for the same period (7%). However, there has been an increase of over 12,000 people (10%) since the census was taken in 2011. This indicates that the city is continuing to see a pattern of steady growth. Job opportunities within the city is one reason that the population is increasing.

Exeter University has two campuses right in the centre of Exeter, which houses a large student population of 22,540. This means that students make up 17.5% of the whole town's population.

Due to this Exeter has a much younger population for those aged under 30 years old at 42.6% than the national average of 37.2% for England.

ECONOMY AND GROWTH

Exeter generated £4.085 million of gross value added (GVA) in 2015, with the increase of 4.3% on the previous year. In 2015, Exeter's GVA per head was £32,090 which is much greater than the national average of £25,367.

During the ten years from 2005 to 2015, GVA in Exeter increased by nearly 30% from £3.152 million to £4.085 million.

In terms of employee jobs, Exeter is the largest district in Devon with 92,300 people working in over 4,000 businesses and accounting for 30% of all employee jobs in the county. It attracts a workforce that extends beyond the district boundary to take advantage of the large number and diversity of employment opportunities available.

Exeter had the highest number of jobs for every 100,000 working age residents (approximately 103,000) in Devon and also significantly exceeded both the regional and national average. This reflects Exeter's role as Devon's economic core and major city economy.

Over £500m was invested in the Exeter area between 2011 and 2016 and new investments are continuing. Significant sums have been used to improve the area's infrastructure (roads, cycle paths, new railway stations, improve flood prevention schemes etc.), build new housing, create new university facilities, introduce iconic new business premises and improve sports facilities. Future development plans include the development of the Exeter Bus and Coach Station site, which will introduce a new swimming pool and the building of an IKEA store. Additional developments are anticipated at Exeter Science Park.

Exeter has an International Airport, two railway routes into London (Paddington and Waterloo), major routes by road (M5 to Bristol), 3 Park & Ride schemes and joined up cycle routes within the city. In 2016, a new railway station opened at Newcourt.

PROPERTY MARKET
Last year most property sales in Exeter involved terraced properties.

Property Type	Avg. current value	Avg. £ per sq ft.	Avg. # beds	Avg. 3 bed paid (last 12 months)
Detached	£442,508	£291	3.8	£323,836
Semi-detached	£282,473	£281	3.2	£261,505
Terraced	£249,337	£274	3.0	£2376,612
Flats	£171,694	£288	1.8	£274,500

Exeter, with an overall average price of £271,892 was cheaper than nearby Topsham (£387,929), Exminster (£297,159) and Broadclyst (£293,730).

During the last year, sold prices in Exeter were 4% up on the previous year and 9% up on 2015 when the average house price was £249,383.

According to a report by the National Housing Federation, private renters in Exeter, are spending 45.3% of their earnings on rent.

The Exeter property market is in short supply, properties are getting snapped up particularly quickly, regardless of the market. Property for rent in Exeter is in especially high demand throughout the whole city. There is a wealth of beautiful Victorian, Georgian, and Edwardian period homes, as well as an exciting mixture of 30's, 50's, and 60's style properties dotted around the city and its outskirts. There is a current boom in new homes developments within the city and surrounding areas, making it an exciting time for first time buyers looking to take their first steps onto the property ladder.

According to the City Council more than 70% of HMOs in the city are occupied solely by students. Landlords who rent to students get a higher income from their properties than renting to professionals or families. Landlords say that properties in areas such as St James and Pennsylvania that are closer to the University demand higher rent and, to date, have always been the quickest to be let.

In Exeter the housing stock which may have traditionally been owner-occupied has been increasingly being adapted and re-purposed as HMOs; leading to areas becoming progressively 'studentified'. As this process occurred the areas became less popular to other members of the community, creating streets which were filled solely with students. As a consequence, traditional businesses and amenities, which supported a cross section of the community (such as schools, nurseries and pubs) began to be lost. Residents of Exeter commented that there is an imbalance in their neighbourhoods and that it affects their local amenities. For example, residents of the Pennsylvania suburb of Exeter have seen the closure of their local pub during university holiday periods due to its main clientele being students.

Many overseas students want an en-suite bathroom, something not readily available in Exeter's traditional housing stock;

Exeter has been faced with over-saturation of student HMO's leading to landlords being unable to let properties – the number of landlords we interviewed who had one or two properties said they had struggled to let their houses in the last few years. This became particularly apparent in 2012.

Restricting the number of HMOs in Exeter

As part of its vision to protect areas where the residential balance was becoming lost, the City Council introduced the Article 4 Direction in 2011. This placed a restriction on the number of houses in multiple occupation and the Council agreed to resist plans for new proposals for change of use from family homes to new houses in multiple occupation (HMOs) in wards where 20% or more of the housing were student properties, to combat the growing imbalance in these areas. This affects around 7,000 homes in the north and east of the city. Proposals to extend the area were the subject of public consultation and were supported in writing by more than 140 households. Their concerns were focused on the imbalance created by too many HMOs (housing both students and non-students).

KEY AREAS

Below I have identified 6 key areas of Exeter for professional HMOs. Those are the most popular areas with the most amount of professional households currently available to rent. Although those demand the highest rents, those areas also have the highest competition from other HMOs.

Having spoken to agents, it is worth considering other, less densely HMO populated areas of Exeter especially in the North of the city such as:

- Duryard & St James
- Exwick
- Pinhoe
- St David's

Alphington

Alphington is a former manor and village, now a suburb of the City of Exeter in Devon. The ward of Alphington has a population of 8,682 according to the 2011 census, making it the third largest in Exeter, with the village itself accounting for about a quarter of this figure. It is surrounded on two sides by countryside, with the Marsh Barton trading estate to the east and Exeter City to the north. The Alphin Brook passes around the Northern edge of Alphington. Alphington is on the South-western side of Exeter.

The modern Alphington Primary School is the main educational establishment in the village, Secondary Education is provided by West Exe Technology College and Exeter College.

Although this is one of the most central areas of the city, the commute is very bad due to heavy traffic. This puts professional renters off leading to not much interest in the available properties.

St. Leonards

Perfectly located, St Leonards is one of the most sought-after areas of Exeter. Popular with families and professionals alike, this area is close to the hospital and schools and is within walking distance of the city centre. This makes it the most expensive area of Exeter.

Architecturally, the area is home to plenty of gorgeous Georgian, Edwardian and Victorian properties. Although beautiful, the properties are very difficult to convert to HMO's.

St Leonards also offers a range of properties to rent. The general area of St Leonard's is served well by public transport; all of the main city bus routes can be accessed throughout.

Pennsylvania

Pennsylvania is a suburb situated on the high ground to the north of the city of Exeter. Its southern slopes, nearest to the city, include many spacious late Victorian and Edwardian houses, while on the steep higher hills, heading north out of Exeter, the housing is mainly 1920s–1970s, with a few newer estates on the city's extremities.

Its proximity within walking distance of Exeter University has made it popular with academics and students.

Heavitree

Heavitree is an historic village and parish situated formerly outside the walls of the City of Exeter in Devon, England, and is today an eastern suburb of that city.

One of the most highly sought-after areas of Exeter, Heavitree offers both the convenience of close proximity to the city centre, as well as easy access to the M5 and the A30. With its own high street, this area enjoys many amenities. Heavitree is a popular choice for a wide variety of buyers, especially those working at the Royal Devon & Exeter hospital and the Met Office which are both nearby.

As with many of the areas in Exeter, there are a wide range of styles of housing within Heavitree. There are many examples of 1930's semi-detached properties with generously-sized gardens which makes them a very popular choice for families. There are also some post-war properties, a converted drill hall, modern properties and bungalows.

St Thomas

St Thomas (St Thomas the Apostle's) is a large 3,700-acre (15 km2) civil parish in Devon, on the western side of the river Exe, connected to Exeter by Exe Bridge. It has a number of pubs, places of worship, a couple of schools and a large shopping precinct. The population, according to the 2011 census is 6,455.

St Thomas consists predominantly of terraced housing, which is common in suburban and inner-city areas. This is a very residential area with much social housing. It is not the most popular with young professionals leading to lower rents.

It is worth noting that St Thomas is the most affordable option, but Exeter had terrible flooding recently and St Thomas is the most prone.

St James

St James is a primarily residential area of Exeter, found between Exeter University and the John Lewis end of the City Centre. It offers lots of period and character property. It is within easy walking distance of the City Centre and close to 3 railway stations, so is a big favourite with those looking to enjoy the benefits of urban living.

Most of St James' housing is made up of Victorian and Georgian terraced properties, although there are the usual scatterings of modern and some older properties. Due to the proximity to Exeter University, many students live in this area, which can lead to a vibrant inner-city atmosphere in some streets.

The area is covered by an Article 4 Restriction, which loosely put, prevents any more houses being converted to multiple occupancy properties.

RENT RATIO

Alphington

Room Type	Per Calendar Month (PCM)
Double Room	£347 - £585
Double Room (en suite)	£400 - £550
Double Room (sharing)	£390 - £585
Double Room (sharing + en suite)	£690
Single Room	£368 - £475
Single Room (en suite)	£475

St. Leonards

Room Type	Per Calendar Month (PCM)
Double Room	£340 - £625
Double Room (en suite)	£520 - £555
Double Room (sharing)	£575 - £690
Double Room (sharing + en suite)	£690
Single Room	£375 - £385
Single Room (en suite)	None available

Pennsylvania

Room Type	Per Calendar Month (PCM)
Double Room	£390 - £525
Double Room (en suite)	None available
Double Room (sharing)	None available
Double Room (sharing + en suite)	None available
Single Room	£355
Single Room (en suite)	None available

Heavitree

Room Type	Per Calendar Month (PCM)
Double Room	£400 - £550
Double Room (en suite)	£495 - £550
Double Room (sharing)	£495 - £550
Double Room (sharing + en suite)	None available
Single Room	£320 - £400
Single Room (en suite)	None available

St Thomas

Room Type	Per Calendar Month (PCM)
Double Room	£450 - £550
Double Room (en suite)	£450 - £475
Double Room (sharing)	£500
Double Room (sharing + en suite)	None available
Single Room	None available
Single Room (en suite)	None available

GROSS YEILD

Alphington – Avg. semi-detached = £287,614

Room Type	Gross Yield %
Double Room - £585	12.2%
Double Room (en suite) - £550	11.5%
Double Room (sharing) - £585	12.2%
Double Room (sharing + en suite) - £690	14.4%
Single Room - £475	9.9%
Single Room (en suite) - £475	9.9%

St. Leonards – Avg. semi-detached = £516,932

Room Type	Gross Yield %
Double Room - £625	7.2%
Double Room (en suite) - £555	6.4%
Double Room (sharing) - £690	8%
Double Room (sharing + en suite) - £690	8%
Single Room - £385	4.5%
Single Room (en suite)	None available

Pennsylvania – Avg. semi-detached = £284,959

Room Type	Gross Yield %
Double Room - £525	11%
Double Room (en suite)	None available
Double Room (sharing)	None available
Double Room (sharing + en suite)	None available
Single Room - £355	7.5%
Single Room (en suite)	None available

Heavitree – Avg. semi-detached = £287,063

Room Type	Gross Yield %
Double Room - £550	11.5%
Double Room (en suite) - £550	11.5%
Double Room (sharing) - £550	11.5%
Double Room (sharing + en suite)	None available
Single Room - £400	8.4%
Single Room (en suite)	None available

St Thomas – Avg. semi-detached = £255,367

Room Type	Gross Yield %
Double Room - £550	13%
Double Room (en suite) - £475	11.2%
Double Room (sharing) - £500	11.7%
Double Room (sharing + en suite)	None available
Single Room	None available
Single Room (en suite)	None available

ROOM-LETTING AGENTS

Hellier Ridley Ltd - Sales and Lettings
Contact: Ben Ridley
Telephone: 01392 340936
Email: info@hellierridley.co.uk
Website: www.hellierridley.co.uk

First Rate Rooms - Lettings (HMO Professionals) (Torbay)
Telephone: 01803 500511
Email: email@firstraterooms.co.uk
Website: www.firstraterooms.co.uk

Exeter Property - Lettings
Contact: Ken & Ruth Blackburn (Owners)
Telephone: 01392 462462
Website: www.exeter-property.co.uk

Inspired Homes - Lettings
Telephone: 01392 347100
Website: www.in-homes.co.uk

Hunters - Sales and Lettings
Telephone: 01392 340130
Website: www.hunters.com/about-us/offices/exeter

Smart Estate Agents - Sales and Lettings
Telephone: 01392 905906
Email: exeter@smartestateagent.co.uk
Website: www.smartestateagent.co.uk

From my research, Exeter appears to be a very good city to invest into professional HMOs. The demand is definitely there. The great transport infrastructure allows the HMO investment to be spread out throughout the city.

It is worth considering the less densely professional HMO populated and cheaper areas especially on the North side of the river. For the below there are not many professional HMOs available currently on the market. The demand is definitely there, especially for couples sharing. So, whether it's because there are not many professional HMOs in those areas or because they are so popular, the rooms do not stay long on the market. The best areas to invest in appear to be:

- Exwick
- Heavitree
- Pennsylvania
- Pinhoe
- Priory
- St David's
- St Loyes

The areas to avoid appear to be:

- Duryard & St James - Article 4 restrictions apply, not possible to create new HMOs.
- Alphington - not popular due to high congestion.
- Mincinglake & Whipton - not popular as it is not a very nice area of the city.
- Newtown & St Leonards - too expensive with period properties making it hard to convert to HMOs.
- St Thomas - too residential and not as popular with young professionals, is prone to flooding

On average, you are looking at Gross Yield of 11% throughout Exeter, with some areas demanding up to 14%.

Charity – Hestia

The despicable act of human trafficking still exists in this world. An estimated 40.3 million victims are trapped in modern-day slavery. The statistics are as follows:

- 24.9 million were exploited for labour.
- 15.4 million were in forced marriage.
- There are 5.4 victims of modern slavery for every 1,000 people in the world.
- 71% of trafficking victims around the world are women and girls and 29% are men and boys.
- 30.2 million victims (75%) are aged 18 or older, with the number of children under the age of 18 estimated at 10.1 million (25%).
- 37% victims of trafficking in forced marriage were children.
- 21% victims of sexual exploitation were children.
- 16 million (64%) forced labour victims work in domestic work, construction or agriculture.
- 4.8 million (19%) persons in forced sexual exploitation.
- 4 million (16%) persons in forced labour imposed by state authorities.
- There were more than 5,000 recorded cases of human trafficking in the UK in 2017.

I work as a volunteer with Hestia. Hestia is one of the largest providers of domestic abuse refuges in London and South East and the main organisation supporting victims of Modern Slavery in the capital. They provide high quality support for adults and children in crisis across London. Working in collaboration with local authorities and partners, they strive to ensure that everyone within their care is equipped with the tools necessary for a life beyond a crisis. I do motivational works shops at their various safe houses across London, I also bring awareness to this charity through my personal and professional contacts, raising funds for their safe houses and support systems.

Hestia
www.hestia.org

Professional Endorsements

Some people want problems to be solved - others like Ersin Sirer want to be part of the solution and actively engage in making bad situations better. Ersin has been a powerful advocate for the work of Hestia for the past 3 years and is actively involved in our work to enable people in crisis to rebuild their lives and realize their ambition. Through his motivational speaking, his mentoring of staff and service users as well financial support and engaging his networks to support Hestia. Ersin shows compassion, courage and commitment to enabling people in crisis to recover and rebuild their lives.

Patrick Ryan
CEO
Hestia
www.hestia.org

Hestia is one of the largest providers of <u>domestic abuse</u> refuges in London and South East and the main organisation supporting victims of <u>modern slavery</u> in the capital.

Ersin has a wealth of knowledge and experience within the property investment, development and construction sectors. He has a firm and well considered understanding of these often complex and volatile arenas not only in the UK but internationally.

Simon J Rose
Managing Director
Meadway Homes
Construction
www.meadwayhomes.co.uk

Representing Ersin Sirer and his company Sirer Global Investments was a pleasure. Always willing and open to ideas we were able to create together interesting Marketing & PR campaigns for his projects and of course the proof was in the publicity generated. The projects that he brought to market were all finally tuned properties with extra special attention to detail, whether in London or the Home Counties, Ersin's expertise always shone though. A truly professional property developer with the added bonus of time and charm spent entertaining journalists made this client a PR dream to work with and converted into many column inches!

Charly Spry
CSPR
Public Relations

I have enjoyed working with Ersin on numerous investment projects over the years and had the pleasure in seeing his business flourish. However, his success will come as no surprise to those who know him, his attitude and approach to business embraces innovation and continuous improvement. Ersin's unwavering motivation and passion has held him in good stead, he strives to find solutions to any complexities and has the ability and resolve to overcome challenges. He has a vision of the future and always keeps 'one eye' firmly looking towards it! Ersin's entrepreneurial spirit has been crucial to his success; he has a natural willingness to assume risks in order to develop his business ventures, his irrepressible ambition is matched only by his relentless dedication to succeed.

Robert Winterhalter
Director RJW Financial Ltd. Finance Brokers

Ersin Sirer has been known to me for over 10 years and during this time I have in the capacity of his Bank Manager assisted in the finance of a good number of his residential development projects.

I regard Ersin as an astute businessman, who has an excellent eye for detail to ensure that the projects he is involved with are consistently finished to an excellent quality and standard. Ersin also possesses a quality of building long term relationships with his suppliers, from co-investors, professional advisers, such as lawyers, bankers, architects through to building contractors. This ingredient has benefited his success to-date and will serve him well in future projects.

Sukhdev S. Dhillon
Director
RSD Associates Limited
Financial Services

I had the pleasure with working with Ersin on a site he developed in Weybridge, from the first meeting it was clear Ersin had a sharp business brain but was also prepared to be advised and guided where appropriate, absorbing information on the local market place, like any good investor or developer the requirement for information, statistic and detail was critical.

I have enjoyed working with Ersin, his easy-going nature but astute business acumen makes it an enjoyable two-way relationship.

Adam Burlison
Partner
Knight Frank

I met Ersin through a mutual friend some 15 years ago and ever since we have remained very good friends as well as business partners.

What I admire most about Ersin is his modesty and honesty. We have travelled many times together on business and for pleasure and you can always sense both his work ethic as well as his witty sense of humour.

In our business dealings, he has always been very thorough in his due diligence and that definitely gives me that extra level of comfort when investing with him. I trust his judgement entirely and have not regretted it.

Over the years, Ersin has amassed a wealth of knowledge in the property field and I am absolutely positive that whoever reads his book will gain a lot from his experience and wisdom.

NK
London
Investor Partner

Having met Ersin as an accidental Landlord, we found a corporate tenant for his superb, newly constructed family home, whilst the sales market wasn't as fast paced. Dealing in business with a true professional like Ersin, over the past couple of years, has been a delight.

Congratulations on your new publication and I look forward to working with you for many successful years to come!

Bea Piazza
Associate Director
John D Wood & Co.

I have known Ersin for well over 15 years. A truly remarkable property genius. Anything he touches turns to gold. The secret I have deduced is his ability to FULLY understand the market he is investing in, to fully analyse and the ability to spot an opportunity.

A.S.M
London
Investor Partner

I have known Ersin Sirer since 1992. Initially I worked in one of his establishments but then bought one of his restaurants in Battersea, London. That's how we started our professional relationship as a tenant and landlord.
I have to say since the beginning of the process I have been treated with honesty and fairness. I have also invested in his projects. He has always been very professional and so far, I have only good words to say about him.
In my opinion he is reliable, trustworthy and competent businessman.

K Bellaqa
London
Commercial Tenant and Investor

I have had the pleasure of working with Ersin for a number of years and can only say what a rarity it is to find such a charismatic, fair person, with a strong moral compass in business. It makes it a joy to work with a person with strong ethical beliefs in the business community which in turn results in building strong long-term business relationships.

Sonia Duggal
Insurance Broker
Director
M & S Duggal Ltd

My Firm has been instructed on behalf of Ersin Sirer who has since become a trusted client and friend. Ersin has proven to be the consummate client; giving clear and unequivocal instructions and, not only understanding the commerciality of the deal but also how the legalities fit into that.

Alex Vlachos
Partner
Lee Bolton Monier-Williams Lawyers
London

I have known Ersin for several years, we were involved with several large residential projects, key property funds were willing to back his proposed development schemes.
He has always come across as a straight talking, responsive, professional businessman with tremendous knowledge of property investment / development and has a large network of business contacts.
He carries out his work in a transparent and morally upstanding way, I am looking forward to reading his book and our continued business relationship.

Nihal Weerasinghe
Managing Director
FSP Consultancy Ltd
Financial Services
London

Working with Ersin is a pleasure - his knowledge and awareness of the markets he works in are excellent. He's always considerate of the need to deliver high standards of each element of a project - from initial concepts and business proposals, through to the marketing; branding, websites, photography and brochures, all the way through to the finished physical product.

David Good,
Web Designer
dngood@gmail.com

Mr Ersin has been a very good landlord since we started trading our business in his building more than 1 year ago. He is professional, helpful and trustworthy landlord. He is always trying to guide or help us whenever we encounter any problem or difficulties. Nowadays is hard to find a very understanding landlord like Ersin, he has been very supportive of our business and always be there when we need him. In addition, he comes to our restaurant one or twice every few months to ensure everything goes well and update us any information that we are supposed to know as a tenant. Overall, he is an amazing landlord and we are lucky to have such a great landlord.

Stefano Arrigoni
Chef Owner
Commercial Tenant

My partner and I rented our flat from Mr Ersin Sirer nearly 2 years ago and have been happy tenants ever since. It is a true pleasure to have a landlord just quite like Ersin. We have always had a smooth and fluid relationship and on the very few occasions when some repairs had to be carried out in the flat, he was always prompt and engaging. He always goes that bit of extra mile to make sure everything is ok. Thank you, Ersin!

Ms A.C.
Residential Tenant
London

I was introduced to Ersin by a business colleague for potential properties work about 5/6 years ago. Our first meeting was at the Chelsea Bun. Over this period, I had the privilege to get to know Ersin both as a business colleague and also as a friend. Over many years business, I have discovered many unethical, dishonest & greedy business people. And that is one thing that I have been very impressed with Ersin and admired. In businesses he is professional and exudes integrity. As a friend he is generous and thoughtful. And on top of all these, he is compassionate and always loves to have the opportunity to give back. Ersin also became my "Go To" person if I ever came across any interesting projects, activities or ideas, as he is always open minded to give time to listen. I was working for a charity called Hestia, who looked after people with mental health, domestic violence and modern-day slavery. Without fail, Ersin supported this charity and often went to the safe houses and refuge to offer workshops on business and self-confidence and even treated some of these people to a Christmas lunch at the Chelsea Bun, which was such a big treat for these people. I knew Ersin from the days before he had children, and I have watched to see Ersin became a wonderful father and family man.

So, in all, I feel extremely blessed that our paths crossed, and I can count on Ersin as a friend and a business colleague and professional.

D T Boyd
London

I have had the pleasure of working with Ersin on-and-off for more than ten years and have always found him to be a sincere and reliable person with an impeccable work ethic. As a client, he is always sure of what he wants and excellent at communicating this to you; as a person, his empathy and fortitude are second-to-none and this combination of factors has always made him a joy to work with.

Matt Reynolds
Photography

It is with pleasure that we can reference our experience working with Ersin. Our experience with Ersin is in the sourcing and development of residential property projects. The success of these endeavours is in no small part attributable to Ersin's enthusiasm, thoroughness, integrity and commitment to seeing things through to completion. Whilst offering opportunities, the property sector can be notorious for the 'interesting' characters one may encounter along the way, highlighting more the pleasure of working with Ersin given his experience, straight up nature and commitment to doing things the right way.

We look forward to working with Ersin for many years to come and wish him every success.

ME and CH
Investors
June 2019
London

I have known Ersin Sirer for many years and we have worked together on several interesting projects together . Ersin is a very straightforward person to work with courteous and clear in his vision of what the end goal is to be. Working with Ersin on his developments is and will continue to be a great pleasure and creatively very rewarding for an Interior Designer such as myself ... Thank you for being included. Best Paul...

Interior Design Consultancy
PSW Design

It's been almost 2 years that he was a guest speaker at an auction which I attended. As soon as I saw his profile on the screen, I was urged to meet him and introduce myself. Since then we stayed in touch and I have started to know him better. And now I can easily say that his businessman profile depends on strong and honest personal values and character. With his beautiful family, Ersin Sirer is not only a successful businessman but also a great father, a friend and also a mentor to me but most important he is a great person to know.

Kerem Hattat
Businessman & Investor
London

I have known Ersin for the past 3-4 years and he has always maintained a very thorough approach to his review of property developments. From a funders perspective he is a model client who always takes a professional approach in his dealings with both us and our advisors.

Neil Moy
Head of Property Finance
Senior Lender
Ratesetter

I have enjoyed working with Ersin Sirer over the last few years on a variety of development projects. He has extensive knowledge of the market and development finance. He is proactive, focused and pragmatic and ensures that all parties work together in progressing and completing transactions in good time.

Harriet Thornton
Partner
LCF Law

I was a residential tenant for two years at one of Ersin's properties in SW London. I found him to be a responsible and caring landlord, always quick to respond to any of my requests and respectful of my peaceful enjoyment of my residence. He treated me as a client not just a number, my needs as a tenant were always met with 100% satisfaction.

Olga
Residential Tenant
London

Working with Ersin? A few words which spring to mind, business minded, knowledgeable, true to his word, hardworking, understanding, dedicated for the great goal, family man, helpful to others, broad minded and creative. In short an incredible and inspirational person.

Rodney Sharp
Director
Zing Homes & Vivid Energy Group Ltd

I have had the pleasure of knowing Ersin since June 2014 when through a mutual business friend, I was approached to price up a new build project in Weybridge Surrey. Subsequently after Ersin purchased the plot, our working relationship started with my company winning the new build contract for two large luxury houses.
Throughout the build period he was scrupulously honest, straight forward in his communication, and always paid our invoices on time, I can honestly say it was a pleasure working with him. Subsequently we have together looked at several larger scale new build residential projects and I am looking forward to being doing business with him again soon.

Simon Redington
Managing Director
www.redridge.uk.com
Redridge Construction

Do You Want To Learn More - Please check my website **www.sirerglobalgiving.com**, for coaching, mentoring, consultancy, events, webinars, books, and more.